Sweeter than Candy

A Hunter's Journal

By Paul F. Vang

For Tim,
thinks for your
service to our MA,
And catching fish.

Oct 22 2018

Dedication

To Kay: After 50 years there aren't many secrets left and I might as well tell the world I love you as much as ever.

I'll also spill the beans and let out the secret that you love our Labs as much as I do. It goes without saying that your love is returned.

Acknowledgements

Some of the stories in this book were previously published, in somewhat different form, in newspaper columns in the *Montana Standard* and *Butte Weekly*, both of Butte, Montana, or the now long-defunct Internet magazine, Gundogs Unlimited.com.

I must express my appreciation to many people who, over the years, kept telling me, "You should put your stories in a book." I hope these stories are worthy. Also, thanks to friends and fellow writers Ted, Chuck and Jerry who read my manuscript and gave me many valuable, if sometimes painful, comments, and especially to Nick Gevock for taking on the challenge of editing and the final shaping of the manuscript.

6240 Saint Thomas Dr.
Missoula, Montana 59803
www.FiveValleysPress.com
info@fivevalleyspress.com

Library of Congress Control Number: 2011939079
International Standard Book Number: 978-0-9835442-4-1

Table of Contents

No Adventures – An Introduction

"I sure envy all the adventures you've had."

I wasn't ready for the comment. I was the guest speaker at a Kiwanis meeting where I was going to plug the annual banquet of Trout Unlimited. I'd brought some props along; a couple fly rods and my fly-fishing vest, and was getting my toys organized. I probably mumbled something along the lines of, "I've had a lot of fun times."

A couple years earlier, after retiring from a long career with the Social Security Administration, I began writing a weekly outdoor column in our local daily newspaper. I'd written about fishing and hunting, but didn't think I'd written about many adventures.

Of course, you have to understand that I define an adventure as an outing where things go wrong—drastically wrong in worst-case scenarios. I've had few of those adventures.

If you define adventure as does my dictionary, as 1: an undertaking usually involving danger and unknown risks; or 2: an exciting or remarkable experience, I haven't had many adventures.

I consider myself a pretty ordinary guy. I grew up on a farm in Minnesota, went to college, got married and raised a family, and spent a whole lot of years pursuing a career in a government bureaucracy. That's hardly the stuff of adventure.

Like most people, I was shaped by my parents. Dad wasn't a hunter, but loved fishing, so fishing was my introduction to the outdoors—the outdoors that didn't have anything to do with cows, pigs, or planting and harvesting crops, that is.

My first six years of public school education were in a one-room country school. During the fall, some of my schoolmates would open their lunch boxes and pull out a pheasant sandwich, leftovers from the previous night's supper. I couldn't think of anything grander than having a pheasant sandwich for lunch, and vowed that when I got old enough I'd hunt pheasants.

Sometime around age 14 or 15, my parents gave their blessing to pheasant hunting, and on the opening day of pheasant season, my mother took me to town and the local Gamble's Store. The store clerk pulled a full-choked 12 gauge single-shot shotgun off the wall and said this was what I needed to get started. He put a box of #4 shells next to the gun, my mother wrote out a check for something like $25, as I recall, and we went home.

The season opened at noon, and on the hour I walked out the back door of our farmhouse, and headed for the fields. I actually had a shot at a rooster pheasant that afternoon. The big, gaudy bird flushed from my feet, scolding and squawking. After recovering from the shock and surprise, I cocked the gun and fired, my first ever shot with a shotgun. I didn't hurt the pheasant, but the recoil of the shotgun almost knocked me over.

A humble beginning, but over the years I've spent a lot of time hunting and fishing. Throughout my government career, involving six duty stations in Iowa, North Dakota and Montana, I was never too far away from some decent hunting and fishing. Still, most of the outings over the years have been on weekends, or on annual family vacations. I've had many quality experiences, but not many I'd classify as adventure.

If I consider my outings over the years as modest, I will concede that I've had a fair number of them. It hasn't always been easy, as each relocation meant learning what the hunting and fishing possibilities were in my new area. About the time I had things figured out and developed a network of hunting spots, it was time to move again and I'd have to start over.

"Don't get out much, anymore," is something I often hear from people commenting on my hunting and fishing stories, often with a touch of envy.

We get tied up in other interests, family obligations, or for one of many reasons, just don't get around to those outings like we used to. Sometimes, things are just too tied up with other baggage. One older man, a WWII veteran and a member of our church, told me several times, "I haven't been fishing for over 40 years. My dad and I used to go out all the time, but after he died, I just didn't have the heart for it anymore."

Another person, with whom I did hunt several times, commented after a deer hunt in western North Dakota, a day in which we'd seen deer, waterfowl, pheasants and other game, "This has been a great day. For years, I'd been so involved with getting more degrees, climbing the academic ladder, or raising a family, I'd kind of forgotten what this was all about."

I quietly replied, "I guess we all make time for those things that are important to us."

I do make time for those things I consider important. There haven't been many adventures in my life, but there have certainly been a lot of days in the outdoors.

Part One

Sweeter than Candy

Chapter 1

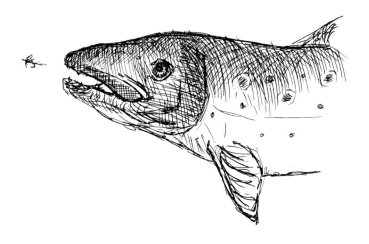

It's September and Anything Goes

"Okay," my wife asks, "just what do you like better? Hunting or fishing?"

"Aw, c'mon," I tell her, "Give me a break. You know the line from the old song, 'If I'm not near the girl I love, I love the girl I'm near.'" At this point, I shut up. Things can only go downhill from here.

Fortunately, I live where I'm close to both hunting and fishing, and in early autumn, I make a point of doing both. Our upland seasons open on September 1, and my wife and I make a point of getting in several 'cast and blast' camping outings, particularly on Labor Day weekend. There are never any guarantees, but always possibilities.

A stroll up the canyon from our campsite in a favorite Forest Service campground often produces ruffed grouse, and a stroll the other direction puts me on a Montana trout stream. A drive up the mountain on a nearby Forest Service road might mean blue grouse. Moose, bugling elk, and bighorn sheep often add a bit of spice to the outings.

Here are some glimpses from some season openers.

When we think of the mountains, we think of cool water and brisk mountain air. Sometimes it actually works out that way.

Then, there are times when summer doesn't want to give up. One year, Labor Day weekend saw record-breaking temperatures in the 90s every day. There wasn't a hint of a breeze, and dust hung in the air. I'm not a hot weather fan, and neither is my black Lab, Candy. Try long-distance running wearing a fur coat and see how you like it.

Fortunately, even in a heat wave, it usually cools off at night, and at 7 a.m., it was a refreshing 42 degrees as the sun came over the mountain ridge to the east. Candy and I quietly entered the creek bottom jungle up the canyon. A cow moose and her calf trotted off at our approach. After a long walk, a grouse flushed on the wrong side of a brush patch. I wasn't ready and the bird was gone before I had a chance to react. A moment later, however, another grouse took off. This time I was ready and I swung on the bird and shot. The grouse fell, and I congratulated myself for collecting a ruffed grouse on the first shot of the season.

The next morning, Candy and I drove up the mountain in search of blue grouse. We stopped to walk a likely area but saw no grouse, but did spot a wild turkey running back into the timber. We drove to the top of the ridge, and walked down an old logging trail.

Three blue grouse flushed and I swung on one of them, dropping a large, mature bird. When I put it in the back of my vest, it felt like I was carrying a couple bricks. The ruffed grouse of the day before was just a chick compared to this big blue.

We made several more walks through the brush, and by 10:30 a.m. I had my limit of three grouse, all big blues. The sun is blazing down on us, it's blistering hot and all I want to do is head back to camp for shade and cool water.

Candy had just become part of our family the previous autumn. A precocious pup, she started retrieving ducks at four months. This, however, was her first serious introduction to upland bird hunting, and a good opportunity to start connecting that summer's retrieving games with her life's work.

A few years earlier, heat wasn't a problem. My shooting was. My hunting partner was a veteran old chocolate Lab, Alix. During our walk up the canyon, she flushed a grouse, giving me a hard right to left quartering away shot. I gave it a two shot salute, and the bird went on its way unharmed.

Back at the campground's non-shooting safety area, a ruffed grouse flushed from tall grass at the campground gate. It flew off with Alix in hot pursuit. While I'm laughing at the situation, another grouse gets up from the grass and perches on the wooden rail fence at the edge of the campground. Alix came back from her run and flushed still another grouse, plus the fence sitter, and then six more grouse flushed from a nearby pine tree. I actually picked up a rock to throw at a bird still perching in the tree, but it turns out that I can't throw rocks any better than I can shoot.

The next day was chilly and overcast, and on our morning walk I bagged one grouse from a pair that flushed. That afternoon, I went to the river for some flyfishing. A bitter wind was blowing from the north, and a sudden snow squall moved across the canyon. I retreated to some brush along the stream, and while I huddled there, I saw trout rising on the other side. Catching fish is more important than comfort. I tied on a dry fly and in the middle of the snowstorm, I caught and released a cutthroat trout.

Bitter cold greeted me the next morning (when we got home that afternoon, I found out that it had dropped to 18° and my tomatoes were frozen and dead). It was so cold that morning that even the grouse wanted to come into camp and get warm. When I stepped out of our tent trailer, two ruffed grouse flushed just feet from me.

I saw more ruffed grouse in that canyon that year than I ever saw before. There must have been a banner hatch. Usually, I see a few grouse, and if I'm lucky, I'll take one or two, and leave the rest for seed, and hope that nobody else even knows about these ruffs. Of course, the net effect was the same. I took one or two birds and left the rest for seed.

That's how it went last year. I got a ruffed grouse and a couple Franklin grouse. Now, there's a fool hen. The trick in hunting Franklin grouse is to hurry up and shoot while the bird jumps from one limb of a tree to another, or is on its way from the ground to a tree branch. Sportsmanship can sometimes be surprisingly challenging.

Fortunately, if the hunting is sometimes inconsistent, early September's fishing often makes up for it.

My favorite time for flyfishing is when most everybody else is coming in, and then I'll fish until it's too dark to see anything.

Once on the river, I forget about frustrations with grouse, as I concentrate on the challenge of figuring out what kinds of insects might be emerging and if the trout will accept my imitations.

On one of those evenings, I went through one fly after another, trying to find something that appealed to the fish, with little action to reward my efforts.

Flyfishing is supposed to be a quiet, contemplative sport. Sometimes, it's difficult to feel contemplative when the fish aren't paying attention. Nevertheless, I called a 'time out,' and called Candy over to join me while I sat on a log to watch the river bottom in the fading light of the sunset. Two white-tailed deer walking through the brush on the other side of the river rewarded our break.

The evening light was quickly fading, and I changed flies once more, tying on a soft-hackled Pheasant Tail Nymph, a pattern developed by Sylvester Nemes, and one of my favorite flies. I moved downstream to a favorite pool.

I settled into a rhythm of casting my fly across the stream and letting it drift down, and taking a couple steps downstream after every few casts. I thought, "If something doesn't happen pretty soon, I'm going to get skunked." No one counts on me to bring fish home for food, thank goodness, but I hate to go out and not catch anything.

I checked my fly to make sure it wasn't fouled with moss. It was fine, but I noticed a wind knot in the tippet. Ordinarily, I'd clip off the tippet and tie on a new section of monofilament. But, it was almost too dark to do that now. Besides, if the fish aren't biting, a wind knot is no problem.

On my next cast, a good fish hit my fly. It doggedly held its place in the stream, resisting my pulling and tugging to get it moving. Finally, it began to run, and took out line. I played it for several minutes, putting on as much pressure as I dared, for fear of breaking my tippet. Finally, the fish tired and I pulled it into the shallows, and slipped the hook out of the jaw of the fish, a beautiful 14-inch Westslope cutthroat trout.

I thought, momentarily, that I should quit right then and there. Catching that cutthroat trout was such a perfect way to end an otherwise frustrating evening. Two casts later, however, another trout hit my fly, and when I landed it, it looked like a twin to my first cutthroat trout. "What a beautiful fish," I told Candy. She wasn't impressed. All trout look pretty much the same to her.

In spite of what Candy thinks, a native Westslope cutthroat trout is a beautiful fish, especially in early autumn, when their bellies are a rosy pink, next to the red slashes on their lower jaw, that give cutthroat trout their name. Westslope cutthroat trout are just barely hanging on in many of their native Montana waters, and are often considered a candidate for the endangered species list. It's an extra thrill to catch a nice 'cut' in one of our rivers where they still thrive.

After releasing the fish, I made one more cast, and there was a vicious rise to my fly, and this time my tippet snapped at the wind knot. Another fisherman was walking the shoreline and offered me the use of his flashlight while I tied on another tippet.

I thanked him and said, "No, I think I'll just call it a night." It was dark as I stumbled back downriver and crossed the stream to return to camp.

Grouse in the morning and trout in the evening. It's hard to improve on that combination, especially when using a fly such as a soft-hackled pheasant tail nymph. With a body made from pheasant tail fibers, and hackle from a Hungarian partridge feather, it seems that on days such as this, this is where it all comes together, and hunting and flyfishing become, simply, different parts of a whole. It's hard to separate one from the other, as one activity seems an extension of the other.

"How was fishing?" my wife asked when Candy and I emerged from the dark back at our camping trailer. I thought just a moment. "Great. A perfect evening."

My woolgathering about past seasons is interrupted by my wife's question. "So, what is it? What's better, hunting or fishing? Make up your mind."

I mumble something about it being time to feed the dog and escape out the back door. It's September, and the bird seasons have started. The fishing is great. I don't have time for any more dumb questions. The shotgun and flyrods are packed and my dog is ready for anything. So am I.

Chapter 2

Ruffed Grouse Misadventures

What do we think of when ruffed grouse hunting comes up? We probably think of the hills and worn-out mountains of New England. We visualize mixed bags of grouse and woodcock, staunch points by English setters and birds flushing from behind old stone walls or from under old apple trees marking where farms were abandoned in the 1800s. One of my favorite hunting books is *New England Grouse Shooting* by William Harnden Foster. It's a wonderful look at the traditions of grouse hunting from a time gone by.

Then, there's my grouse hunting. There's not much poetry left by the time I've spent a day in the aspens.

Of course, I've had disadvantages. I've never hunted grouse in New England. I'm originally from Minnesota, which is one of the major Great Lakes area ruffed grouse states. However, I grew up in farming country. Pheasants thrived in Dad's cornfields but we were a long way from ruffed grouse.

Actually, I might never have gotten started hunting ruffed grouse if a long-ago Saturday morning had been a little warmer. We were living in northeastern North Dakota at the time, and my son, Kevin, then age 13, and I were heading out in search of some late season mallards. A cold wave had come through, dropping overnight temperatures to near zero and the wetlands were frozen solid, the waterfowl gone south.

Feeling discouraged about hunting prospects, we took a dusty back road for the trip back home. I noticed a wooded valley that cut through the flat prairie farming country. I found a side road going down to the valley dead-ending next to a brushy creek bottom. I suggested that perhaps we could find some rabbits.

We hadn't gone too far into the woods when our black Lab, Sam, picked up a hot scent. Suddenly there was a thundering "Whirr!" of wings and a gray bird rocketed from almost under our feet and disappeared into the timber. "What was that?"

We went through a mental checklist. It obviously wasn't a duck. There weren't any pheasants in that country. Certainly wasn't a rabbit. Sonofagun, it had to be…a ruffed grouse!

We continued to explore the wooded valley and we were pleasantly surprised to flush several more grouse that afternoon. This defies conventional logic, but in what many consider the quintessential prairie state, North Dakota, I got hooked on hunting ruffed grouse. Over 25 seasons have come and gone since then. Sam hunted grouse with me until a few days before she died at age 14, and her successor, Alix, a chocolate Lab, learned her trade in North Dakota aspens and when I transferred in my job, she transferred her skills to the mountains of southwestern Montana. Candy, a two-year-old black Lab, is my current partner.

Over the years, I've had many adventures with my Labs as we've explored the hills and the aspens in search of ruffed grouse. Sometimes we've come home with grouse, our absolute favorite game bird on the dining room table. Then, there are days when all I bring home are excuses and stories.

The valley where we first found grouse continued to be a favorite grouse covert for many years. Along the creek, aspens and alders grew thick as hair on a dog and walking through it was nearly impossible. But grouse were often there so we walked it. Kevin and I were struggling through the brush, one day, when a grouse flushed. The trees had shed their leaves and the bird headed, in plain sight, across a clearing. I raised my gun and swung on the bird for the perfect shot. As I pulled the trigger, the end of the gun barrel hit a tree and my swing stopped. The shot pattern ripped a divot of bark from a tree. The bird kept flying.

Actually, when I think about it, there are many trees scattered across two states with broken branches, shattered trunks, and scarred bark marking where it sacrificed itself for a ruffed grouse.

Alix was in her third season and still learning her trade. We spent the morning hunting ducks and then stopped to hunt grouse on the way home. Alix moved into an aspen stand and suddenly there were birds flushing. It sounded like a squadron of B-17s taking off. Then I saw wild turkeys emerging from the trees. Finally, birds stopped flushing and Alix came back to me, red-eyed and foaming at the mouth. "Did you see those birds?" her face asked. "They were big as bombers!" She was trembling with excitement. I thought she'd never be the same after that encounter.

Later that fall, we were hunting on Thanksgiving weekend. Snow had fallen earlier but melted. Kevin, now out of college, was home for the weekend, and we took advantage of this opportunity to go grouse hunting. It was cloudy, daylight was fading and we had temporarily lost our bearings. Finally, I figured out where we were and we started trudging back to the truck through the gathering darkness. By the trail, snowshoe hares were 'hiding' from us. The bunnies had completed their fall changeover to pure white winter fur, but relied on sitting perfectly still to make themselves invisible. They virtually glowed in the dark.

Habitat that produces ruffed grouse is also prime habitat for big game. Over the years, chasing moose out of the aspens has gotten almost routine, if seeing half a ton of long-legged moose go crashing through the trees can ever be routine.

White-tailed deer frequently appear during our grouse hunts. Usually, the encounters produce the sight of a deer's tail raised high as it disappears into heavy brush.

On one hunt, I found myself face to face with one of the biggest whitetail bucks I've ever seen. A mysterious encounter was when I could hear a deer moving away in the brush. The brush didn't seem thick enough to cover the deer, but somehow the deer slipped away unseen until it decided it was safe and then I just got a glimpse as it exploded up a draw. I'd bet that deer also carried a good set of antlers. I often wondered where those big bucks went when the deer season opened.

One day, a forkhorn white-tailed buck popped out of the hillside brush patch that Sam was working. The deer ran down the hill and across a creek when it literally bounded into the middle of a covey of Hungarian partridge. Huns were suddenly in the air all around him and the deer almost jumped out of his skin with panic after his surprise encounter with the partridge.

A Montana ruffed grouse hunt often has the possibilities of a mixed bag with blue grouse and Franklin grouse sometimes sharing the same mountain. One near-perfect afternoon's hunt produced a big blue grouse from atop a mountain ridge, and after we climbed down off the ridge to follow a creek back to the truck, Alix flushed a ruffed grouse that I added to our bag.

More typical was the following week, when I hit several favorite spots but bagged nothing. As the sun was setting, I came home, hot, muddy and exhausted, just in time to see my wife, Kay, coming out the back door with a camera in hand.

A neighbor had called and asked, "You want to see a grouse?" A blue grouse had wandered down from the nearby mountains and into his urban backyard where it was happily eating berries from his hedge.

I wanted to get a fishing net and capture the grouse, since I apparently couldn't get them any other way. Kay asserted that the neighborhood was sanctuary.

Chapter 3

Blues

"Just how in the blue bloody heck did you find this place?"

The Watercress Covert is on the edge of a county highway and a lot of traffic goes by there, but aside from the occasional teenager stopping to drink beer (I pick up their aluminum cans) I didn't think anyone else ever stopped on this wide spot on the road.

My impulsive thoughts remained unspoken. Instead, I smiled and said, "Hi!"

My uninvited visitor grinned and asked, "Are you through hunting?" I was, having just spent the last couple hours slipping and sliding around in new-fallen slushy snow.

He let a springer spaniel out of his compact SUV as he put on a brown vest and uncased a shotgun. He was from Bozeman and said he'd heard about ruffed grouse hunting in this area, and decided to see if he could find some birds.

I finished loading my stuff in the back of the truck and commanded Candy to kennel as I opened the truck's rear door. I told him I'd seen no birds. My visitor seemed to be a nice guy and I wished him well, though I felt like telling him it probably wasn't wise to wear a brown vest in this area while the elk season was still on.

In fact, in almost 20 years hunting in southwest Montana, with many days dedicated to ruffed grouse every autumn, this was one of the few times I ever saw another hunter in my coverts. As best as I can determine, I'm one of the few hunters in my area that specifically looks for ruffed grouse. I usually pick up my shotgun shells after shooting, so if I see shotgun shells on the ground I know that another hunter has been there. I seldom see any. Empty .30-06 cartridges are much more likely.

If you talk to hunters who are actually out for upland birds in the early season, chances are that they are after sage grouse or blue grouse.

Sage grouse are a great game bird, to be sure. I had my introduction to sage hens years ago when I had a chance to hunt on a neighbor's ranch along the Powder River in southeastern Montana. John Moore, my boss at the time, and I combined for a Saturday's hunt for sharp-tailed grouse. We'd already gotten a bunch of sharptails, but on our way out of the ranch we spotted a flock of sage grouse along the trail. We got out of the car and approached the big grouse. They were reluctant to fly but finally some took off. I shot, bringing down one or two birds, as I recall, and added them to the day's bag.

Back home, I cleaned the birds and added them to the freezer, anticipating future game dinners. After we finally had a sage grouse dinner my wife told me in no uncertain terms, "You don't need to bring any more of them home."

I took the hint. When we moved back to Montana and people asked if I hunted sage grouse, I'd just smile and say, "My wife and I made a deal many years ago. If I didn't bring any more sage hens home, she wouldn't throw any more out." Most people nod in understanding, though some offer recipes for turning sage hens into a culinary delight.

Previous years in prairie country prepared me for sage grouse but not blue grouse. I knew ruffed grouse and my first few years of living in mountain country included a number of outings dedicated to getting to know the area and identifying ruffed grouse habitat. Blue grouse presented a different challenge. People talked about hunting blue grouse, though all too often their stories centered around finding an old dead snag on a mountainside where blues liked to roost and then shooting them off the tree with a .22 rifle, being careful to shoot them from the bottom up. Presumably the sight of their dying brothers and sisters falling by them might spook other birds. This bird behavior caused the op-ed page editor of the newspaper for which I was then writing to frequently refer to blue grouse as "the wily fool hen."

So, I figured I'd just keep hunting ruffed grouse. It was something I knew about and understood. Once in a great while I'd get a blue but I couldn't take much credit—it was just an unlucky bird bumping into a lucky hunter. When people asked me, "Have you seen many blues?" I'd generally try to change the topic of conversation, or admit, "Well, I've never really figured them out."

One day at coffee, we had a discussion about game birds and when the discussion turned to favorite bird for eating I didn't hesitate. "It's the ruffed grouse. There's no question."

My friend and occasional hunting and fishing partner, John Banovich, said, "Oh, no. Blue grouse are better." When I looked at him questioningly, he explained, "They taste just as good as ruffed grouse and they're two or three times bigger."

When September came we planned a grouse trip. I had retired from the Social Security Administration the previous January and during lunch on a day of flyfishing on the Big Hole River the topic of blue grouse came up. We talked about getting out for blue grouse, preferably when we didn't have to worry about bow hunters. His pithy comment was, "Now that you're through ****-ing around at the Social Security Office, we can get out in the middle of the week."

John remembered a mountain near the Big Blackfoot River where he had successful blue grouse hunts in past years with his sons. I picked him up at his house in pre-dawn darkness. It was just getting light when we turned off the blacktop and started going up the Forest Service road to "Chicken Ridge," as he called it.

We slowly drove up the gravel road, negotiating many switch-backs to the top of the mountain. About three-fourths of the way up we spotted a large blue grouse walking along the road, picking up gravel. "There he is. It's your bird," John said. "Go get your gun and just walk up on him. He won't fly."

I went to the back of the truck and got out my shotgun and loaded up. The bird was nervous and started walking away as I approached, and the faster I walked the faster he walked. Finally I raised my gun and shot the bird on the ground. It staggered but didn't fall. Before I could give it another barrel, it went off the road, into the second growth cover down the hill. I called to John to let Alix out of the truck, figuring she'd have an easy retrieve.

Alix picked up bird scent in some logging debris at the side of the road and followed it down the mountainside. Then the bird took off with a roar of wings, disappearing as it flew off into timber far below.

I walked with Alix, empty-handed, back to the truck. John gave

me a hard time about the grouse, "I guess I need to give you a lesson on ground-sluicing birds."

We finally got near the top of the mountain, below an old clear-cut ridge that John said was always a good spot for blue grouse when he used to hunt here 30 years ago. We hiked to the top of the ridge and all around the area, but we never saw another grouse the whole day, though on the way back down the mountain we did find a patch of huckleberries and on the way home we picked chokecherries along a trout stream.

The next year we took another trip to Chicken Ridge. It was 8:15 a.m. when we got to the top of the mountain road. Though it was early September it was a damp and chilly morning and a light drizzle in the air welcomed us back to Chicken Ridge. We parked the truck and start walking up the hill, taking time to watch a mule deer doe. The deer stood still, staring back at us, trying to figure out what we were. After we started moving again, the deer bounded off.

We worked our way to the top of the ridge where John and I decided to split up for the walk back down the brushy old clear-cut.

When I got back to the truck, having not seen any birds, John was still nowhere in sight, so Alix and I stopped for a rest. After a drink and a cookie I decided we should look around. We walked into some trees across the road from where I had parked and Alix picked up some bird scent, just as a grouse flushed out of range. Then a second bird flushed and I got off a shot at it. I saw feathers drifting in the air after the shot, but the bird kept on flying. Alix and I worked our way to the top of the next ridge, but I wasn't too enthused about going down the steep slope, so we walked back to the truck. Along the way, Alix picked up a scent and came back with the grouse I had shot at earlier, dead as a stone. John was back at the truck when we got there. He didn't see any grouse, but did see another deer and an elk at the top of the ridge.

After the walk, John, who is 10 years my senior, admits being bushed. On the way home he says, "I walked my rear end off up there," adding "I figured that would be the last time I'd ever walk to the top of that mountain."

There is rain in the air as we started walking another draw near the bottom of the mountain and before we got back to the truck it changed to snow, big blobby flakes of snow that quickly soaked my jacket and vest.

When I got home late that afternoon I decided I'd better cover the garden. It was a good thing I did because it got down to 28° that night. My tomatoes, beans and zucchini were nipped by frost but survived.

A biology note. Blue grouse in Montana and other inland mountain areas are now officially known as dusky grouse to distinguish them from a slightly different blue grouse in Pacific Coast mountain ranges. These birds are referred to as sooty grouse. I suspect most hunters will continue to call them blue grouse wherever they find them.

If that early September hunt was cold, it was hot on Labor Day weekend, two years later. Alix was gone by then and Candy was just a year old and starting her first season of hunting.

We were camping at a Forest Service campground near a well-known western Montana trout stream. Just above the campground is a creek bottom that holds ruffed grouse, and on our first morning in camp I dropped an immature bird with my first shot of the season and Candy retrieved the first ruffed grouse of her career. I always feel good when I drop a bird with my first shot of the season. If I missed another shot a few minutes later I still had a .500 shooting average. In baseball that would be more than good enough to get into the Hall of Fame.

After breakfast it was already starting to get hot. Afternoon temperatures had been in the 90s all week and there was no relief in sight. Still, I decided that Candy and I should take a drive up the mountain road near the campground in search of blue grouse. In previous years I'd drawn a blank, but you never know.

On the drive up the mountain we didn't see anything but on the way down I spotted three blue grouse along the road. I got out of the truck and with gun in hand walked up on them. I got a shot when they flushed but the birds kept flying. Normally I'd start hiking off in their direction but by now it was just too darned hot for walking. In fact, I spent the rest of the day in the shade, reading the latest Tom Clancy thriller. You know it's too hot when it's too hot to fish.

The next day, I headed back up the mountain, and my second walk in the woods resulted in two heavy birds in my hunting vest. A couple walks later, and I had my day's limit of three blue grouse. The day after that, I flushed birds on every walk that I took, even though I ended up with just one grouse. I began looking over different areas and thinking, "Looks like that should have some grouse." I'd check it out, and sure enough, Candy would pick up a scent and flush a bird or two.

The outing was instructional. I was beginning to understand blue grouse cover and was also finally beginning to understand the passion others have for the Wily Fool Hen, though after several hunts I have trouble thinking of this bird as a fool hen. A grouse that takes off with a thunder of wings, dodging its way through the trees, frustrating hunters, dogs, and shooting skills, isn't a fool hen.

After mornings of stalking the Wily Fool Hen, I'd return to camp weary, soaked with sweat, with sore feet, and running low on shotgun shells, realizing I'm no longer a candidate for the Hall of Fame. Candy, though just a rookie, looks at me with disappointment when she flushes a bird and I miss. Yes, these fool hens are true grouse.

If I thought from that opening weekend of 1998 I finally was reaching an understanding of blue grouse, I was just setting myself up for disappointment. The following few years the mountain seemed as devoid of blue grouse as it was full of them that year.

2005 was another good blue grouse year and if Candy learned what it really means to be a bird dog with blues, we both learned more about blue grouse this year. For the first time in several years we were finding grouse on just about every walk. Even a well-accepted belief about blues was holding true, "Walk the meadows below the tree line early in the morning. Grouse like to feed in early morning, picking off frozen grasshoppers from the sagebrush. "

We got into birds on every day of that opening weekend, and in cleaning the birds I made another connection. Most of the birds had red berries in their crops. The plants that had red berries aren't out in the sagebrush; they're found in the timber. When walks in the sagebrush didn't produce grouse I started looking in the timber and found more grouse.

On the last walk of the Labor Day weekend Candy and I walked up a steep hillside. It was tough walking but we found the ground cover full of berries. My hunch paid off when Candy put up a grouse. I shot and Candy made the retrieve. While I was paying attention to Candy's retrieve another grouse flushed from just a few feet away. I turned, made a hurried shot, but missed.

We ended the holiday weekend with six blue grouse in all, and if I hadn't missed some shots I could have had more. I later consulted a field guide to Rocky Mountain plants and wildflowers and found the red berries. The berries are the fruit of the whortleberry, sometimes known as 'grouse berry.' "Find grouse berries," the book says, "and you'll find grouse." Sometimes it works; sometimes it doesn't.

So, after experiencing occasional successes with blue grouse have blues replaced ruffed grouse as my favorite game bird on the table? That might be stretching it a bit. Nevertheless, whether ruffed or blue, a grouse dinner by candlelight is a special occasion.

Chapter 4

Opening Day

Over the course of the season, there are many opening days. In Montana, most people think of the opening of the big game rifle season as Opening Day. For me, it's the opening of the pheasant season. The sleep of many Montana hunters is haunted by the prospect of a bull elk stepping into a clearing at first light. My dreams are filled with the sight of long-tailed pheasants taking wing, rousted out of hiding places by a Labrador retriever.

Opening Day means a road trip to eastern Montana and a farm along the Yellowstone River. I've been returning to that farm just about every opening day for 16 years.

I first went there the autumn after moving back to Montana, tagging along with Morrie, my father-in law-and James, my wife's sister's husband. Morrie's age and health eventually caught up with him (he died in 1999), and James seems to have lost interest in upland bird hunting. I keep returning.

Pheasant hunting is an old pursuit, not much changed in the last century. Other technologies, however, keep evolving in ways unimaginable just a few years ago.

We used to get permission to hunt private property by knocking on farmhouse doors. We still do that, but once rapport has been established, technology takes over. The last few years we've been exchanging emails during the summer, just to let our farm friends know I'm coming.

In August, I sent Deb, the farmer's wife, an email confirming that I'd be there on opening day. She replied that she'd be gone that weekend, but that there seemed to be lots and lots of birds around. I replied, "Keep them fat, dumb and happy."

The farm is a river bottom property that borders the Yellowstone River, going up to a benchland overlooking the valley. Sugar beets are a principal crop, along with corn, hay and other crops. A network of irrigation ditches divides and separates the fields. A large irrigation canal that serves the irrigation 'project' goes through the farm, as well as a railroad track. It's intensively farmed, but the farming practices leave lots of fence corners, brush lines, and brush patches.

The valley has always had abundant wildlife, but today's variety would astound Captain William Clark, who floated by here back in 1806. The Lewis & Clark journals often refer to pheasants, but they meant grouse; sharptails, sage grouse, and further east, the pinnated grouse, better known as prairie chickens. Pheasants weren't successfully introduced to the United States until 1881, when Judge Owen Denny, serving as American Consul General in Shanghai, shipped 28 pheasants to his brother's farm in Oregon's Willamette Valley.

Eastern Montana became pheasant country after the Federal government established irrigation projects along the Yellowstone River, settled families on 160-acre farms, and dared them to make a living.

A lot of dreams were shattered in the process, but the farms eventually consolidated into economically viable units, and pheasants found easy living along the abundant edge cover of the projects. Whitetail and mule deer, which always lived there, continue to thrive, and wild turkeys, another transplant, are the new kid on the block. Canada geese loiter along the sandy bars of the river and mallards, teal and wood ducks thrive in old oxbow pools near the river.

The sun is up, but it's still chilly when I park my car on the edge of the field on opening day morning. Candy and I start our hunt by climbing to the benchland above the valley. The farmer feeds cattle there in the winter months, and it's full of weed patches, with several brushy draws that lead back to the valley floor. Pheasants could be anywhere.

We don't push any birds from the tall weeds, but when we get to a long brushy draw, Candy goes into the cover and suddenly birds are flying. I pick out a rooster that came up scolding and pull the trigger. The bird goes down, and Candy scrambles up to the top of the bank to retrieve it. After putting the bird in the back of my vest I glance down at my watch. It's 8:03.

Candy goes back into the brush and puts up a young rooster. I can clearly see its colors, though, and I shoot again. It's 8:08 a.m., and with two shots we've collected two thirds of our limit of three cock pheasants.

A lot of people talk about the 1940s as the "good old days" of pheasant hunting. I'm sure they were right, but for me, the good old days of pheasant hunting are right now.

As we walk along the bench, a couple more birds flush wild, and I miss a long shot at a rooster. We stop back at my parking place for a drink of water and to get rid of the pheasants in my vest. The weight of a pheasant or two in the back of a bird vest is one of those wonderful feelings that only a bird hunter can really appreciate, but it's still a relief to shed that weight.

There's a long creek bottom bordered by an railroad embankment on one side. The creek also serves as a drainage ditch, draining excess irrigation water from the field on the other side. Every few years, someone comes in with a backhoe and cleans out the ditch of debris, such as beaver dams, cattails and other efforts of nature to make it natural. The backhoe has been dumping the mud and debris into what has become a long 10-yard wide strip of brush, trees and weeds.

Pheasants feed in the field and nest and relax in the brush line. If danger threatens, it's a short flight over the creek and railroad embankment where they're safe—for the time being, anyway.

I try to keep Candy at my side as we walk to the far end of the brush line, but she must be catching the hot scent of pheasants, as she suddenly charges off and the air is full of pheasants.

I get her back under control and we start working the cover. Pheasants are flushing from the top of the railroad embankment, but I can't do anything about them. One cock bird flushes from the edge of the creek, heading for the tracks. I swing and shoot and see the bird drop. Candy goes over for the retrieve but comes up empty. I send her back, again and again, to search the brush, but to no avail. The creek is too wide and too deep for me to cross, so after Candy finally refused to go yet another time, I regretfully declare the bird lost and we move on.

When we approach a bend in the brush line, a spot that usually holds pheasants, birds flush, going in all directions. I have a hard time picking out a target, but finally pick out a rooster for a quick right to left quartering away shot. I hit the bird, but it appears only lightly hit. The bird lands in the top of a tree. I fumble with shells, planning to dispatch it before it takes off. Then the bird falls down, finally catching in a branch several feet off the ground. I walk over and pluck the dead bird from the branch. I glance at my watch. It's 9:33, and we have our limit of pheasants.

It isn't always this easy.

On September 18, 1992, my wife told me, in the morning, that we were going to go shopping after work. Our wedding anniversary

28

was on the 16th, so figured it had something to do with that. When we stopped at the sporting goods store, I thought she probably had a new fly reel in mind. We walked past the fishing displays, though, and ended at the gun counter. She said, "Pick out a shotgun."

It didn't take a lot of debate. I'd had my eyes on the Ruger Red Label 20 gauge over/under shotgun for several years. As it worked out, it was the only 20 gauge O/U they had in stock but, happily, one was enough.

In retrospect, I should have headed for the local gun club and shot a bunch of clay pigeons with that new gun. I did go grouse hunting a couple times, but didn't have any shooting opportunities.

On October 17, my 53rd birthday, the pheasant season opened and I was in my favorite spot.

There were plenty of birds, and I emptied the gun a couple times within the first couple hundred yards of our walk, all to no effect.

I wasn't worried. If I was sure of anything the first minutes of our stroll, it was that there were a lot of birds that year.

I was developing a new style of hunting. Alix, my chocolate Lab, and I would push up a draw and we'd put up birds. In one brushy draw, my adrenaline took a jump when Alix nosed out a trophy class whitetail buck and a doe. Still, when it came to pheasants, my morning's vocabulary seemed to be, Bang! Bang! "Damn." Or for variety, Bang, Bang! "Shit!"

By now, it was about 10 a.m., and my confidence was thoroughly shaken. I was afraid of something like this and, just in case, had brought my trusty old Weatherby Patrician 12 gauge pumpgun along. Alix and I walked back to the truck and traded guns and swapped out the remaining 20 gauge shells for 12-gauge ammo.

Things were settling down by now, and we weren't seeing the large numbers of birds we'd seen earlier. I had a shot at one bird, and it seemed like I winged it, but Alix wasn't able to find any sign of it.

After a lunch break I dropped one pheasant that landed in a plowed field. It landed on its feet and was off to the races. I tried to anchor it, but it kept on going and Alix wasn't able to catch up with it. Finally, back in the draw where we'd pushed the big deer a few hours earlier, I hit a bird solidly, and Alix had an easy retrieve.

At the end of the day, I was exhausted. Trudging across a cattail slough, I tripped on a hummock and fell flat on my face.

I stopped at a game warden's check station on the way back to town that evening. One of the wardens seemed astonished, "That's all you got?"

I didn't do any better the next day of the opening weekend, getting just one sharptail grouse that wandered into the riverbottoms.

A footnote to that markedly unsuccessful weekend is that Alix seemed to have developed an eye infection. I took her to the veterinarian after we got home and he retrieved an inch-long weed seed that had imbedded itself in her eye.

When things go wrong, it often seems that they stay wrong!

A year later, the Ruger and I are old friends, and what a difference a year makes!

On opening day, the ground is wet and muddy from rain showers that fell overnight. I'm hunting by myself, again, though I find myself sharing the area with another party of four hunters with two dogs. I watch them work their way across the bench. I have a brief conversation with one of them who says they haven't had much action.

After they've gone by, Alix and I work our way up a brushy draw, where the other party had crossed earlier. We flush one rooster and drop it, and Alix makes the retrieve.

Coming down the next draw, another pheasant flushes, giving me a quick but effective shot. Alix was down in the bottom of the draw and missed all the action. It was an easy walk to pick up the solidly hit pheasant and put it in the vest. Alix finally came back to me, and got all excited when she came to the spot where the bird flushed. She came back, several times, to sniff the area before I was able to get her to move on.

We move into an area of dense brush where Alix flushes another rooster and I make a good shot. Alix retrieves the bird and I glance at my watch. It's 9:30—definitely one of my faster limits.

I'm back in town at 10:30 and my mother-in-law comes out from the house and asks, worriedly, "What's wrong?"

I'm pleased to tell her, "Nothing's wrong. I just had my limit and had to quit."

Thinking back over the years, there have been a lot of opening days, along with the growing realization that I have a lot more opening days in my past than are likely to be in my future. There have been productive days and some I'd rather forget. I've been fortunate in that I've gotten to be one of the lucky few people who don't have to worry about where to go on opening day.

Actually, I have to confess that I have missed a few opening days when I've had conflicts I couldn't duck and had to open the season a few days or even a week late. I've still had my share of success, but there's something about being out there when it all begins.

If it seems I've had more than my share of shooting success in recent years, it's one of those things that came relatively late in life. I can recall some pheasant hunts of over 40 years ago when I got in on the last couple years of the pheasant abundance of the old Soil Bank program in eastern North Dakota. I remember seeing a lot of birds, but the birds I brought home and put on the table were few and far between, or the result of hunting with other guys and a sharing of the bag at the end of the hunt.

Practice, including lots of clay pigeons along with years of hunting, plus having a gun that, after an awkward first season, is like an extension of my body, all go together to make me a pretty decent wing shot. Not perfect, by any means, but with the help of a good dog and matured shooting skills I've had some great opening days.

Thinking of those opening days of years ago, I often recall one opening day. There were four of us who worked together at the Social Security Office that made plans to hunt on the opening day. On Friday morning, Bill called in sick. The rest of us speculated whether he'd be okay the next day, with George, the eternal pessimist, positive that he'd be out for the weekend.

Nevertheless, at Oh-dark-30, the next morning, when we pulled in front of Bill's house, Bill came out with his hunting gear and piled in the car. "I thought you were sick," one of us asked.

"I wasn't that damn sick, for Pete's sake," Bill snapped back.

Opening Day

Chapter 5

Candy is a Pheasant Dog

She's resting and loafing on her dog bed, but Candy is a happy dog. She spent the weekend doing what she was born to do, and that's hunt pheasants.

Last weekend marked the beginning of the 1999 pheasant season, and we celebrated in eastern Montana, with our son, Kevin, and brother-in-law, James Vogele. Kevin and his family came over from Minot, North Dakota, and he splurged on a Montana upland bird license so he could hunt with us, as well as enjoy a family reunion.

The weekend was one of transitions. Two years ago, Kevin joined us for the opener, and at that time, my old chocolate Lab, Alix, was in rapidly declining health, though able to have one last great pheasant hunt. Kevin's black Lab, Nikki, looked relatively young, at the time, in comparison to Alix, and I was envious of the hunts that Kevin and Nikki still had to look forward to. It was on that same weekend that we made the connections to purchase Candy, then an 11-week old puppy, and bring her home.

This past weekend we again saw the wheel turning. Kevin's Nikki is now the old grizzled veteran, over 12 years old, and clearly declining. Kevin and his family recently acquired a new puppy. Kate is a four-month old yellow Labrador retriever. Like all puppies and small children, she's cute and lovable. Being cute and lovable is the principal survival skill that puppies and children share. If it weren't for that, they'd never survive puppyhood or childhood.

At age two, Candy is in her second full season of hunting, and if there's anything she understands, it's pheasants. She has figured out that pheasants love thick cover, and when we approach a jungle of thorns, burrs, and weeds she looks for a way in and if there are pheasants in that jungle, they're soon flying for a new hangout. If I'm standing in the right place at the right time, my 20-gauge over/under shotgun barks a command, and surprisingly often, I'm calling on Candy to retrieve a pheasant.

While it's not in her training, and it certainly wasn't suggested as part of her breeding, Candy also often points pheasants and grouse. In the Labrador retriever world, there is controversy as to whether Labs should point, that is to lock up in mid-stride; indicating there's a bird in close proximity. I really think it's more of a matter of finding a tight-sitting bird than anything else. Still, by the standards of the American Pointing Labrador Association, she's a pointing Lab.

George Hickox is a nationally known dog trainer, and I had the opportunity to chat with him at a conference and asked him about pointing Labs. George was emphatic in his opinion that if you, as a hunter, want a pointer, you should buy a dog with centuries of breeding for pointing. "The strong point about Labs," he continued, "is their ability to mark and retrieve, and the fad for pointing Labs is just that—a fad."

Nevertheless, when Candy goes on point, as she did several times over the weekend, with both Kevin and James as witnesses, I must confess I feel like a father whose children bring home report cards with straight As. It isn't necessarily part of the contract but I'm awfully pleased and proud.

The tough part of owning a dog is watching them age. During the first couple years you have a dog, you're anxious for them to learn some skills and manners, and to settle down enough so you can tolerate having them around. Then, almost overnight, they're a senior citizen, with a gray muzzle, and a gimpy hitch in their stride after a weekend of hunting.

I looked back at my hunting diary entries for 1987, and on Nikki's first pheasant hunt, she was just a puppy, but still managed to flush three pheasants out of cover that Kevin, Alix, and I had already walked through. On that same weekend, Alix retrieved a Hungarian partridge that I managed to hit, and when she was bringing it back, Nikki jumped up and bit off the bird's head.

This past weekend, Nikki found some birds, but after the first hour of hunting, would mostly tag along next to Kevin. At day's end, she was content to lie down and rest her weary bones in the late afternoon sunshine. Kate welcomed us home and delighted in the smell and feel of feathers. We'd throw her a pheasant wing for her to retrieve; though a whole pheasant was still too much for her to contemplate.

Candy is entering the prime of her life. Nikki is reaching the end of her career, and Kate is running around the yard playing with a pheasant wing. Being able to visualize the future is a mixed blessing.

Chapter 6

Welcome to the Jungle

I call it "The Jungle."

It's a strip of land bordered by a railroad right of way on one side and an irrigation canal on the other. It's on the eastern Montana farm where I've enjoyed hunting privileges for a number of years.

Except for a small alfalfa field at one end, it's a disused part of the farm. There are cottonwood trees and several cattail sloughs, but the bulk of The Jungle is brush. Some of it is what we call "buckbrush." There are also Russian olives, wild roses, and hawthorns.

There are a few trails going through The Jungle where cattle and deer have gone. The buckbrush is waist high and it's relatively easy going. The thorn thickets, on the other hand, are almost impenetrable. If I were to take a motorized vehicle into The Jungle, I'd choose a tank.

The reason I go there is pheasants, though it's a court of last resort. When the easy and more obvious hotspots have been hunted and I need to find a pheasant in the worst way, I head for The Jungle.

It's never a sure thing, though. I can't recall many times when I've hunted The Jungle when my dog hasn't put up birds. Getting shots at birds is something else, however, as often the wily roosters will get up from the other side of a clump of brush. I hear the rush of wings and, sometimes, a scolding cackle, but I can only stand there in frustration as the bird flies off, unseen.

There have been other times when we've put up a lot of birds, but all out of range.

Sometimes those old roosters make mistakes. One year, 1993 as I recall, needing just one more pheasant to complete my limit for the day, I elected to go into The Jungle. Alix, my old chocolate Lab, was with me. She picked up the scent of a pheasant that was cornered between Alix and me. I missed the bird when it flushed, but I dropped the bird cleanly with the other barrel.

On a recent hunt the birds were acting scarce, so it was time to go back to The Jungle. It had rained overnight so after just a few minutes of walking, I was soaked as was Candy, as she led me through the buckbrush and thorns.

As we approached the end of The Jungle, I had to move out because the brush was so thick. Candy was still in the thick of things, however. As I stood on the outside looking in, I could hear Candy crashing around. Then I heard birds flush and saw a rooster pheasant clear the top of the brush, giving me a quick shot. I shot and saw the bird fall.

Following the momentary feeling of exhilaration for making a tough shot, I thought, *Oh my gosh, how will we ever find that pheasant?*

Candy came out of the brush, not having seen the bird fall and wasn't anxious to go back into the thorns. I found a path into the brush near where I thought the bird went down and when I could go no farther, I told Candy, "Go get the bird." She looked at me as if I was crazy, but dutifully went snooping through the thorns. She came back empty a couple times, and again I told her, "Go find that bird. We've got a bird in there."

I could do nothing but encourage her. I could hear her moving in the brush, sniffing and struggling. Occasionally, I heard splashes when she went slogging into the cattail slough. I sadly entertained the thought that we might have to give up on this pheasant. Back in the days when we hunted pheasants without a retriever, it seemed like we lost more birds than we ever brought home. It's hard, but almost inevitable.

My dark thoughts were interrupted when, this time, Candy emerged from the brush with a soggy pheasant in her mouth. I don't know whether the bird was wet from the rain or if it had fallen in the slough. All I knew was that, miraculously, she found the pheasant.

It was the only pheasant of the day, but the seventh, and most memorable, of the trip. Over three days of hunting, she flushed every bird I shot at and retrieved every bird I managed to drop.

I don't know if Candy understood why I was hugging her. *All in a day's work*, she seemed to say. *Let's go hunt up some more birds.*

Chapter 7

Deep Freeze Mallards

It's 15° below zero and I'm walking into a North wind. Snow crystals hit my cheeks, reminding me that my face isn't quite numb—yet. I stop and turn, to let the wind attack my back for a moment, while I wipe frozen tears from my eyes. I ask Candy, "Are we having fun, yet?"

If bitter weather bothers her, she doesn't show it. We're in search of ducks, and if we're hunting, she's happy. It's all I can do to keep her at heel while we approach the little spring creek that crosses the pasture we're walking across.

We approach a bend in the creek and I release Candy, "Flush 'em up, girl." She runs to the creek bank. Suddenly the air is full of mallards. I pick out a greenhead from the flock, and I swing my 12-gauge over/under and shoot. The bird drops and I pick another and shoot again. Another duck drops. In a few minutes, Candy has retrieved the birds and my vest has the reassuring heft of a pair of prime mallards, and I don't feel cold anymore.

I should confess that there are many times when we've flushed flocks of mallards and haven't gotten anything, or I'll lightly hit one and have to use my second barrel to bring the duck back down to earth. I know other hunters who have told of similar opportunities and after three shots with their old Model 12 have ducks raining down on them. I occasionally get a 'Scotch double,' when I accidentally drop two ducks with one shot, but that's the exception. For whatever it's worth, if I do get a Scotch double on my first shot I generally miss on my second shot anyway.

Winter duck hunting isn't for the timid. If your idea of winter duck hunting is wearing a camo T-shirt and shooting ducks in Mexico, you'd better stay home, because, baby, it's cold outside. But, if you like roast mallard on the dinner table, these winter duck hunts are worth it.

I did much of my waterfowling, over the years, in the pothole country of North Dakota. It's legendary duck country, but in most years, the action is pretty much done by the end of October. In a typical year, the deep freeze hits the prairie country around the first week of November and the ducks are gone, possibly entertaining well-heeled hunters down in Arkansas. Of course, with global warming hitting even the prairie pothole country, that late-season shooting occasionally gets extended these days.

Now I live in southwest Montana and spend October and most of November hunting upland birds. The ducks can wait. In November and December, arctic winds begin to roar down from Canada, and when northern prairies are locked in ice and snow, spring creek duck hunting is just getting interesting.

I had my introduction to sub-zero duck hunting around 40 years ago. My brother-in-law, Jim Vogele, invited me to join him on a December duck hunt. He knew of a shallow warm-water pond near the Yellowstone River in eastern Montana. The weather was bitter cold, with morning lows of -30°, warming to a relatively balmy -15°in early afternoon. We put out decoys and waited.

As the sun began to set, we spotted distant flocks of ducks coming from grainfields on the other side of the Yellowstone. Soon, ducks were pouring into the decoys. Even when we were standing in the open and shooting, the ducks kept coming. The ducks needed water and the river was covered with moving ice floes that would soon solidify into a mass of ice. The river was not a hospitable environment and the pond had the only open water around.

I hunted that pond just that one weekend back in the early '70s, but I'll always remember the fast shooting we had, as well as how miserably cold it was out on that frozen prairie.

Mallards are America's favorite duck. They're big, wary, and if their breeding grounds on the northern prairies have enough water, they're prolific. When mallard family groups start joining others for the trip south, they form flocks numbering in the hundreds, if not thousands. They're also hardy and don't mind cold weather. After all, they invented the down jacket, didn't they? As long as mallards can find food and open water, they'll take all the cold weather that Mother Nature can throw at them.

Geological features of mountain country create something we call spring creeks. Bedrock rises to near the earth's surface, and water in the aquifers comes out of the ground to form springs and spring-fed streams that seldom freeze. Many of them are famous among anglers who specialize in spring creek flyfishing. When winter comes, most anglers are gone, and the creeks become a haven for mallards.

Some creeks have hot-water springs that make the water too warm for trout. In fact, one warm-water creek I hunt has tropical fish that somebody dumped in years ago and managed to survive. One of the adult "boys" on the ranch smiles when he tells of, as a kid, making a relatively easy buck, occasionally, when local residents paid him for netting fish for their aquariums. When the weather turns seriously cold, mallards flock into these steamy 'hot tubs.'

Spring-fed streams aren't confined to mountain country, of course. There are spring creeks in many areas across the country, and we could include the tailwaters of dams on rivers as places to look for winter ducks. Again, as long as ducks have food and open water, they'll handle winter.

Cold weather duck hunting can be rewarding. It does, however, test hunters and their equipment.

Make sure your shotgun is ready for cold weather. A few years back, I approached a creek and when the ducks flushed, my first shot went, "click." I was using a pumpgun at the time, so I shucked the shell out and shot again. This time, the gun went off and I dropped a duck. I searched in the snow for my first shell and found it. It had a dent on the primer, what we might now call a "dimpled chad." In the subzero conditions, my firing pin was just gummed up enough so that it would strike, but not give a good enough hit on the primer to discharge the shell. I had several other shots that morning where I did the same thing. Shoot once to loosen up the action, and then shoot again to actually discharge a shell. If you hunt to relieve stress, this doesn't work.

Incidentally, that old pump gun has spent most of the last 15 years in my gun cabinet. My primary reason for retiring that gun was that I'd gotten used to using an over/under and switching actions was just too confusing for my normally erratic gun-handling. Nevertheless, a shotgun that doesn't reliably go 'bang' when you want it to isn't a candidate for longevity.

Dress for success. This means clothing that will withstand extreme weather and keep you warm and dry. This particularly means boots. If you have the tiniest pinhole leak in your waders, for example, you'll soon know it and your feet will freeze. You can start the day with boots that are intact, but it doesn't take much to poke a hole in them. Bring extra dry socks for emergencies. Duct tape will often work for an emergency repair job. Dress in layers. Sometimes, a day that starts off in minus double digits will be mild and sunny by noon. Then a wind comes up and temperatures plunge. Be prepared.

Actually, on the creeks I've been hunting in recent years I haven't had to use hip boots at all. I walk on dry land and let my dog do the water work. If I occasionally get a boot wet, it isn't the end of the world—as long as I keep moving, of course.

Take care of your dog. I specialize in jump shooting, and as long as we're walking, Labs don't mind cold, even if they've just retrieved a duck and are covered with icicles. On the other hand, if you're shooting over decoys, you might consider a neoprene vest for your dog to help it stay warm. Above all, when the hunt is over, this is no time to let your dog ride home in the back of an open pickup truck.

Occasionally, I've gotten feedback from readers of my newspaper column who tell me that jump-shooting for ducks isn't a sporting proposition. I'm supposed to use decoys and wait for them to come in. I just smile and tell them that I don't have the patience to sit behind a blind in sub-zero weather hoping for birds that might or might not appear. Besides, there are all those sneaks I make and come in at the wrong spot on the creek and see all those ducks flush out of range. Then there are other times when I make too much noise, or my dog gets out of control. There are a lot of things that can go wrong on an approach and I've been a party to most of those screw-ups.

Of course, decoy hunters have their own problems. A rancher friend told of some duck hunters who came in at sunrise to set out decoys on the warm water spring creek that wanders across his property. Something like 400 ducks flushed when they made their approach. They set out their spread of dekes and waited for the mallards to come back in—just as they do in the magazine articles. "They sat out there in the cold until 5:00 in the afternoon—and never fired a shot," my friend related.

Chapter 8

"Gonna' Take a Sentimental Journey"
or
The Thousand Mile Woodcock

"Someday, before I die, I want to go back to North Dakota to hunt grouse," is something I've occasionally said to my wife.

"For goodness sakes, then, let's do it," was her reply this past summer, and so we began making plans for the trip.

The pheasant season opened the second weekend of October and we towed our travel trailer to eastern Montana for the weekend's hunt, leaving it at Kay's sister's house while we went back west to attend to other obligations. A week later we came back, hooked up the trailer and went on to our son's home in Minot. The next morning we were back on the road, driving through steady rain. In mid-afternoon we set up camp in Icelandic State Park in northeastern North Dakota. It had stopped raining and there were still a few hours of hunting time.

I headed to a state-managed Wildlife Management Area that was a favorite hunting spot years ago. It's an area of mixed oak and aspen with an old homestead at the top of a hill where an old log barn gave the covert its name.

The WMA is a half-mile off the gravel road and the trail is one I've driven many times, though never when the conditions were this soggy. I started having second and third thoughts about this excursion. Unfortunately, there was no place to turn around and as long as I was moving I wasn't about to stop.

I got to the entrance to the WMA where, fortunately, grasses provided firm footing for parking and turning around. "We're here," I told Candy, "we'd better go hunting."

As soon as I walked into the soggy woods, I took a deep breath, savoring the earthy smell of soggy, decaying oak leaves. It's funny how that familiar, but almost forgotten, odor can flood the senses and bring back forgotten memories.

A two-hour walk through the woodland didn't produce any grouse, though we did move a couple snowshoe hares and a whitetail buck. I spotted a clump of highbush cranberries and picked a couple hands-full of tart fruit. If my goal for the trip was to find ruffed grouse, a secondary goal was to pick enough cranberries for a Thanksgiving relish.

We emerged from the woods at 4:30 and I elected to hit the road. If I got stuck I'd need to allow a little extra time to find a farmer in the neighborhood willing to pull me out with his tractor. Fortunately, we just managed to get out, though the truck was plastered with black, sticky mud from one end to the other.

The next morning dawned sunny, though dense fog covered the low areas. We had plans to take a side trip to Fargo that afternoon to visit friends, so I had time for just a morning hunt. This time I elected to hunt a tract of woodland that was right on the highway.

In the middle of the area are windrows of downed aspen trees where, evidently, the state bulldozed older aspen trees to regenerate the forest. They were gloriously successful. After many seasons in the drier climate of western Montana, I'd forgotten how dense a young aspen forest can be.

On this walk we moved a couple more whitetail deer and picked some more highbush cranberries. Along the edge of the forest, Candy put up a ruffed grouse and I got off a couple shots but missed.

By the time we finished our circle it was almost noon and time to get back to camp.

We have a successful trip to Fargo that afternoon, getting back to camp around 11 p.m.

The next morning it's a gray, drizzly morning as we drive off to another WMA that I used to hunt.

This WMA is an area of aspens, occasionally broken up by grassland. It's on gently rolling terrain, an area that, after being broken up by homesteaders, blew out and by the time it was taken out of production back in the 'Dirty Thirties' had degraded into sand hills. Mother Nature reclaimed the area with the regeneration of aspens and native prairie grasses. The area is named the Jay Wessels WMA in honor of a now-deceased area farmer and conservationist who was instrumental in getting it protected.

After parking the truck in a spot I remembered from long-ago hunts, Candy and I walk across the grassland and enter the forest. We haven't gone far when I see Candy working some scent in a low spot. I wait, gun poised, to see what's going to come up. A bird flushes. I swing and shoot, and shoot again, dropping the bird on the top barrel of my over/under. Then it occurs to me that when the bird flushed there was a sort of trilling whistle sound. "Was that a woodcock?" I ask myself. Candy finds and retrieves the bird and, sure enough, it's a woodcock.

While woodcock are often the target of eastern upland bird hunters, this is the first woodcock I've ever seen in real life. A few years earlier, North Dakota put "timberdoodles" on the upland bird game list, and in planning this trip I wondered if we might find some. Still, this woodcock was a total surprise.

Half an hour later, Candy leaves a trail and goes into dense cover and I hear the "whirr" of a ruffed grouse flushing. We follow the direction of the flush and I get an easy shot at a big ruffed grouse—and miss.

Not long after that shot we emerge from the trees and I have this uneasy feeling that, in this featureless, foggy and drizzly area I have no idea where we are in relation to where we parked the truck and started our walk. Luckily, I spot the truck off in the distance and we go there to deposit the bird.

We return to the woods, taking an old fire trail through the woods that I remembered from old hunts. On this walk we move two grouse; one unseen in the brush and another that's just a blur as it disappears into the trees.

Although I've been checking my compass regularly I'm beginning to get this uneasy feeling that I'm losing my bearings, again.

I should note that this is a feeling of déjà vu. On another hunt in the 1980s, I set off across the area in search of grouse with Candy's predecessor, Alix. That was a warm and partly sunny day. I don't recall just when I realized something was amiss. Perhaps it was when we emerged from the aspens and looked across at farmland that didn't look at all familiar. After a couple more circles didn't help, I spotted a distant farmhouse and headed for it.

The farmer was amused when I told him about getting lost and told me I was about 5 miles from where I'd parked. He cheerfully gave me a ride back to the Scout.

This time, I emerged from the woods along the main road, about a two-mile walk back to the truck. Along the way Candy detours into a soggy spot and I hear a whirr and a whistle. She put up another woodcock. I follow her in, belatedly, but no more birds come out.

We finally make it back to the truck. We're thoroughly soaked and chilled—or I am, at least. Candy just seems to be enjoying herself, though she doesn't object to getting into the truck for the drive back to camp.

The next morning I have time for another morning hunt. Naturally, as time is limited, the weather is improving a little.

On this walk we don't move any grouse. The morning's highlight is, at the edge of the woodland, hearing ducks quacking in the distance. I see a flock of mallards circling over a distant marsh. They circle, circle, and finally set their wings and head in. I'm waiting to hear shotguns go off, but there is no sound other than the sound of welcoming ducks. Sometimes, it seems, duck calls are the real thing. Amazing—it sounded just like a good caller.

Before finishing our walk I spot a deer and a snowshoe hare. On my four days of hunting I've also managed to pick a couple plastic bags full of highbush cranberries.

I had hoped that this sentimental journey back to the aspen and oak forests of northeastern North Dakota would end with several limits of ruffed grouse. Apparently I picked the wrong year as grouse were apparently at the low end of their cycle.

But all is not lost. After all, I do have enough cranberries for at least two batches of highbush cranberry sauce. I also have a story about a sentimental journey for a Thousand Mile Woodcock.

Chapter 9

Interrupted Season

Over the years I've had a number of hunting partners, ranging from co-workers to friends and acquaintances.

One of them, John Burke, was a small town lawyer, whose office was in the same building as my office. After several years of casual conversations we finally went on a weekend pheasant hunt together and everything clicked. After that weekend we went on several ruffed grouse hunts. By the end of the season, however, I got transferred and was back to hunting by myself. It was a major shock, just a few years after we moved, to get word that John died from a sudden heart attack while shoveling snow. John was a former Army officer, running addict and a nut on physical fitness. He was the last person you'd expect to go that way.

Another John B (for Banovich) was a more recent partner. For several years we spent many days together each season, from early flyfishing to late season waterfowling. Several years ago, his son, an internationally known wildlife artist, moved his home and studio back to Montana and John's focus in life started to revolve around helping his son. It has now been several years since we've gone out for a day of hunting or fishing.

My favorite partner is the one I raised. Kevin started tagging along on hunts when he was six or seven. By the time he was old enough to legally hunt he already had years of experience under his belt. The problem with raising your own hunting partner, however, is that, sooner or later, you have to say goodbye. For several years, we were able to have occasional hunting weekends when he came home from college on fall break, as well as Thanksgiving and Christmas. Then he went off to graduate school in Illinois. After getting his Master's degree, he got on at the Mathematics department at Minot State University in Minot, North Dakota. We had a couple seasons where we were able to get together for hunting weekends—and then we moved to Montana.

Living in adjoining states does give us occasional opportunities to hunt and fish together, though the cost of non-resident hunting licenses makes us think twice about these hunts.

We returned to Minot on the way back from the Thousand Mile Woodcock hunt and we had a weekend for hunting.

On Saturday, it was overcast and rainy when we left town in the pre-dawn darkness. Our destination was a Wildlife Management Area along Lake Sakakawea, the sprawling impoundment on the Missouri river formed by the Garrison Dam.

We left the highway and splashed our way down a muddy road and parked at the first pullout at the WMA boundary. We put some candy bars in our vests, loaded guns and set off into the grasslands. Kevin had his yellow Lab, Kate, and my canine partner, of course, was Candy.

We walked through a couple shelterbelts, where a few pheasants flushed wild, and then headed down a hill to a creek bottom. During high water years, it would be a back bay of the lake, but this year it's back to being a creek. There are dense weed patches along the creek bottom.

At the edge of the creek, Kevin spotted a broken-wing cripple run out of the weeds and into thick cover on the other side of the creek. Candy picked up the scent and was off to the races. A couple minutes later, Candy emerged from the cover with the pheasant in her mouth.

Just a minute or two later, Candy flushed a cock pheasant from a weed patch and I had an easy crossing shot. I didn't miss and at 9 a.m. I had two pheasants in my vest.

We spotted pheasants flying into a distant draw, so we worked our way in that direction. At the bottom of the draw two pheasants flushed in front of Kevin and he dropped the rooster. Kate and Candy collaborated on that retrieve.

We worked our way to the top of the draw and then took a meandering walk through another shelterbelt. While a number of pheasants flushed wild out of the trees we didn't get any shooting.

I should note, at this point, that the WMAs along Lake Sakakawea are heavily hunted, especially this area midway between Minot and Bismarck, North Dakota's capital city. The pheasants that live in this area quickly become educated survivors. Nevertheless, it's a wildlife paradise, with heavy weed and grass cover, brushy patches, shelterbelts and food plots. Furthermore, when the pressure gets too heavy, all the birds have to do is fly across a bay to another peninsula or an island, or simply walk across a road and sit out the weekend on adjacent posted private land.

It's mid-morning, now. The skies are clearing and the heavy cover is drying out enough that our brush pants are starting to dry off. We also see other groups of hunters working the area. Like I say, this is a heavily hunted area.

We work our way back down to the shoreline of the bay where we flush several pheasants, mostly out of range. Kevin does get a couple shots off at a flushing rooster. We're both surprised when the pheasant keeps on flying, going across the muddy backwater, going in the general direction of a knoll on the next peninsula.

We work our way up the creek bottom until we are able to get across the creek. We walk through another shelterbelt and then head for the knoll at the top of the peninsula. After working through a thick weed patch, we get out into the open and see that Candy is worrying a dead pheasant. The bird is still warm, so we're positive this is the bird Kevin shot at half an hour earlier.

We're feeling pretty good about things, now. We're hunting on heavily used public land and we each have two birds toward our three pheasant limit.

I don't have much time for self-congratulations, because Candy has just flushed another pheasant from a weed patch, and I just have time to get off two quick shots, dropping the bird with the top barrel. I have my limit, my first North Dakota pheasant limit since 1987, if anyone's keeping track.

We have a chance to complete a second limit when we knock down another bird. Unfortunately, it's lightly hit and we aren't able to recover it. This doesn't happen often when hunting with a good retriever, but, sorry to say, it's not always 100 percent.

It's a long way back to the turnoff where we left Kevin's truck hours earlier. The skies are now a brilliant blue and the sun is shining brightly on the prairie. I had long since shed my Polar fleece vest and stuffed it in my hunting vest on top of my limit of pheasants.

The dogs are feeling the heat, too. Kate is obviously tired, content to trot along with Kevin. I suggest that he give her a bite of a candy bar, as her blood sugar is probably getting low. We cross the creek, yet again, and both dogs get a good drink of water. When we walk through some thinner cover, I realize that Candy seems to have problems, too. She's holding up her right rear leg as she walks.

We finally make it back to the truck, completing our five-hour walk. We sprawl out on the grass and share sandwiches and apples. The dogs are content to bask in the sun and enjoy a chance to relax.

I feel Candy's leg, suspecting that perhaps she's picked up a thorn in her pads, or, even worse, has fractured something. I can't find anything and manipulating her foot doesn't seem to cause Candy any discomfort, so I'm at a loss as to what might be wrong.

While we still lack one bird for our limit, I suggest to Kevin, "Maybe we'd better go back home and give these dogs the rest of the day off. We can come back, again, tomorrow."

That evening, Candy seems content to spend the evening sleeping and relaxing. We try to see some improvement in her use of that back leg, assuming it's just some sort of muscle sprain.

The next morning it's raining again and Candy seems content to go back to bed in the trailer, rather than whining to jump in the truck for a hunt. That's a serious indication that things are not right.

As it worked out, she didn't miss much. We went back to the same area we had hunted the day before. This time, however, we trudged through the rain and soggy cover without getting a shot. We flushed a few hens in shooting range, and on a hillside next to the bay dozens of pheasants flushed out of range, disappearing off into the drizzle.

By noon, our clothes are soaked and we're chilled to the bone. The temperatures aren't any big deal—somewhere in the mid-40s— but we're both feeling thoroughly chilled. We decide the prudent thing to do is to head back to Minot and watch the Minnesota Vikings game.

A couple days later, we're back home in Montana and we've made an appointment with a veterinarian. The veterinarian, Dr. Laura Wold, one of several vets on the clinic's staff, manipulated Candy's knee joint and made a quick diagnosis, "She has a ruptured ACL (or Anterior Cruciate Ligament). She's going to need surgery."

In addition to the bad leg, Candy has had a recurrence of a chronic allergy problem. She spends most of her time scratching, without much apparent relief. Prednisone is one of the few things that seems to give her relief, so Laura filled a bottle with pills and sent us home, asking me to bring her back in after 10 days or so.

There's another piece of advice I don't want to accept. "She can't hunt anymore," Laura cautioned, "until we get this fixed."

It's advice I'd prefer to ignore, as we had plans to hook up the trailer for one last hunting/camping weekend on Montana's northern prairies. It was difficult the next day, when Bill, the landowner who has graciously let us camp and hunt on his farm, phoned to see if we were still planning to come that weekend. I explained that Candy wrecked her knee the previous week and that I couldn't hunt her.

Instead of towing the trailer up north, we took it to our RV dealer to have it winterized and declared the RVing season over. I spent the rest of the week catching up on work.

A week later, we got up early on Saturday morning. Kay was going to a conference in Las Vegas with several co-workers. I saw her off on the plane and went home. We'd had some cold and snowy weather early in the week but today it was going to be sunny and mild. I did some yard work and then watched Candy moving around the yard. She seemed to be using her leg without apparent pain.

I decided, with my wife not there to tell me we couldn't, to take Candy out for a short hunt. We needed to do it, bum leg or no bum leg.

The elk season was on and a couple elk hunters were parked by a turnout near the bottom of the hillside having lunch. They assured me they had no plans to hunt the aspens, so Candy and I started our walk.

If Candy had a wrecked knee, you'd never know it by the way she ran into the aspens. We hadn't been in the trees more than five minutes, slipping and sliding through patches of slushy snow, when a ruffed grouse flushed, flying straight up the hill, giving me a relatively easy going-away shot. I dropped the bird and Candy made the retrieve of a large, mature brown-phase grouse.

I pocketed the bird and we walked up the hillside, missing a shot when another grouse flushed.

We walked back down the hill and spotted another grouse flush, out of range, from a clearing and flew into a brushy creek bottom. We followed into the brush, not seeing anything, so walked back out on to the trail that circles the hillside. On the other side of the creek bottom, Candy caught a scent and went back into the brush. I tried to follow. The bank was slippery and muddy and I was gingerly trying to get down the bank without falling when the grouse flushed, skimming along the ground, going up the hillside. It was out of sight before I had a chance to swing on the bird.

Continuing down the trail, another grouse flushed. I shot and missed as the bird disappeared into a grove of pines. We followed the bird, almost tripping on an old barbed wire fence hidden in the brush. It looked like this bird had given us the slip when it flushed again. I had just a second to react before raising my gun to shoot. There was an explosion of pine branches ahead of me, but somehow, it seemed like I saw feathers fly.

Candy was off in search of the bird and after a moment came running back with a gray-phase ruffed grouse in her mouth.

I all but gave Candy a hug as she delivered the bird, saying, "Candy, what do you think of that? We've got two grouse!"

It was just a two hour hunt, but the most productive ruffed grouse hunt of the season, especially considering the two thousand mile round trip we'd made a couple weeks earlier with nothing to show for our efforts except one lone woodcock.

A few days later, I brought Candy back to the veterinarian's office. Her prednisone had run out and the itching returned. Dr. Ed Peretti, the owner of the practice, wasn't amused when I casually mentioned that we'd gone hunting that Saturday, and that a casual observer would have never noticed any limping on Candy's part.

"I suspect it's mind over matter," Ed replied and then, with a stern look, said, "Look, her hunting season is over. We have to do something about that leg. She's in pain."

We had plans to go to California for Thanksgiving week, so we made tentative plans to have Ed do knee surgery the first week of

December. As for her itching, he made plans to do allergy testing at the same time as the knee surgery. In the meantime, he prescribed antihistamines to help with the itching while the steroids, which would interfere with surgical healing, cleared out of Candy's system.

I spent the following couple weeks in a dither. On three of those days, I got out my rifle and went deer hunting, never firing a shot, though I had opportunities. I grumbled to myself, "If that had been an equivalent opportunity for a grouse or pheasant, I'd have been shooting."

If I hadn't realized it before, I understood now, more than ever, how much my autumns revolve around a Labrador retriever and hunting. Years ago, I hunted without a dog because I didn't have any choice. After 34 years of hunting with my dogs, I can't go back.

Interrupted Season

Chapter 10

Borrowed Dog

By the calendar it was the first day of winter, though mild, southerly breezes made it seem more like October than December.

After a noon meeting, I had time to change clothes, throw a few things in the truck and head for a patch of public land that's usually good for a pheasant or two each year.

I parked the truck, and let out Kate while I put on my vest and got out my shotgun. When I walked down a little trail into the brush, Kate held back. Maybe dogs can't talk but they certainly do have body language and Kate was telling me, "This is just too weird."

Two weeks earlier, Candy had her knee surgery and was just beginning to recover from that trauma. Ed Peretti, the surgeon, warned me that on a triangular-shaped limb, such as a back leg, it's hard to keep a bandage on. His parting words were, "She'll probably have it off in a few days."

The bandage lasted a few days, but by Friday it had slipped down past the surgical site and Candy, the incurable licker, began licking, opening up the incision. She earned a new bandage covering the resutured incision and a new wrinkle: an Elizabethan collar, or E-collar as veterinarians refer it to. I think of it as a conehead. Candy tells me it's torture.

In any event, Candy was home on recuperative leave.

The night before, Kevin and his family stopped on their way to go to California for Christmas with our daughter, Erin. By prior agreement, we were taking care of Kate. They were happy to leave Kate with us, as four people, along with luggage, Christmas presents, etc., made things tight in the Honda Civic sedan. Both granddaughters were covered with blonde hair from Kate's shedding, so they were really happy to go on without her.

I was happy to see Kate, of course, so I could get out for some end of season hunting. It had been too long since that first weekend of November and that last ruffed grouse hunt. We'd hunted together back in October, so I assumed Kate would be willing to hunt for me.

Kate simply wasn't too sure about this outing. She was happy to go for a ride in the truck but hunting with Grampa—and without Kevin? Apparently, our having known each other since she was a pup wasn't the same as teamwork.

I try to jolly her along and encourage her to get out and work the cover in front of me. She sort of goes through the motions, but it's easy to see that her heart isn't into this project.

The area we're hunting is along a river and two creeks and an irrigation ditch run the length of it. We've crossed the creeks and are working tall, grassy cover along the irrigation ditch. A cock pheasant flushes and, while I'm rusty, not having fired a shotgun in six weeks, I manage to scratch the bird down on my second shot.

Kate isn't sure about this development, but as we walk up to where the bird fell, I can see it lying on the grass. I call Kate over for the easy retrieve. Kate sees the bird and gingerly walks up to it and tries to pick it up—by the beak!

This is too much for the pheasant. He was just lightly hit and in a daze. Being picked up by its beak was just too undignified and he promptly woke up, shook himself off, and without much of a struggle managed to scurry off into tall grass.

Kate followed the bird and a couple times almost had him in her grasp but couldn't quite hold on. I could see the grass waving where the bird was running. I should have shot, but at a range of less than ten feet, it would have been easy to miss and a direct hit? Yuck.

In any event, Kate quickly lost interest in the bird. Again and again I called her back into the cover to pick up the scent trail. Kate half-heartedly went in but quickly lost interest. I sat down with her and tried to give her a pep talk about retrieving, all the while thinking about my black Lab at home. "Candy wouldn't let that bird get away," I told myself.

Finally, sadly and reluctantly, I came to the inescapable conclusion that the pheasant had made his escape. "An easy meal for a predator," I thought. I'm kicking myself for not grabbing the pheasant.

Finally, we moved to another part of the area where Kate actually got on a hot scent and put up a loudly scolding cock pheasant. Willows screened the bird so I didn't get a good shot at it and missed. At least now, however, Kate is getting excited about the hunt and for the next five minutes scurries around the brush in search of more bird scent.

That's the end of the day's action. I'm sick about losing that pheasant and mentally chastising Kevin for not taking Kate hunting more often.

The next day, in somewhat more seasonable winter weather we

went duck hunting. After blowing a sneak on a little bunch of mallards on a tiny spring creek, I'm surprised when we put up five mallards on another section of the creek. I pick out a drake and shoot, with the bird falling on the other side of a fence.

When I get up to the fence I can see the duck lying dead in the grass. I pick up Kate and throw her over the fence to retrieve the duck. Kate looks at me like I'm crazy. So, I climb over the fence and lead Kate over to the duck. She sniffs at it and turns up her nose. I pick it up and throw it out for her. Again, she refuses to have anything to do with it. I finally pocket the bird in the back of my vest, lift Kate over the fence, get myself over, too, and we finish our walk. Meanwhile, I'm reprising my thoughts about Kevin not getting his dog enough exposure to birds to really turn her into a retriever.

A couple days later, and it's Christmas Eve day, and I take a chance on missing the first quarter of the Minnesota Vikings/Green Bay Packer football game for a morning duck hunt.

Today, I make a successful approach on a little bunch of mallards in a spring creek. I even make a double on the birds, with the two drakes falling within a foot of each other. Again, Kate wants nothing to do with those birds. Fortunately, I'm able to jump across the little creek to make the retrieve myself. I briefly consider checking another spot, but pass it up because I know I wouldn't be able to jump across that creek.

I make it home for most of the football game to see the Vikes give the hated Packers too many Christmas gifts. I should have hunted a little longer.

A few days later, it's still December, but the Christmas wrappings are on the way to the landfill and the tree is turning brown and dry. On the bright side, there are still a few days to go before the end of the pheasant season on New Year's weekend.

I'm hunting a creek bottom on private land. It's a mixture of dense willow jungle, tall grass and cattail sloughs. There's an access road above an irrigation ditch that's a virtual pheasant highway, judging from all the bird tracks in the dirt. In a normal year, the tracks would be in snow, but on this mild, late December day there's precious little snow to be seen.

One pheasant flushed wild ahead of us, but I didn't get a good enough look at it to know whether it's a hen or cock. That was the only action of the morning. By the time we completed a circle and got back to the truck it was a balmy 47° and I shed a couple layers of clothes before the afternoon walk.

After working on my tan, basking in warm sunshine and eating a sandwich, we got back to the hunt, making a loop through sagebrush and tall grasses before we returning to the willow jungle.

In a clearing in the willows, Kate flushed a pheasant rooster, and I dropped the bird with my second shot.

The bird fell, without a wiggle, in light cover, but nevertheless I was overjoyed to see Kate run over and pick up the bird and proudly bring it back to me. I praised her no end, telling her what a good girl she is.

That was the last pheasant of the season. I was out a couple more times and on a New Year's Eve day hunt, with snow falling and the temperature in seasonable single digits, I had a shot at one pheasant. Unfortunately, I was daydreaming when the sole shoot-able pheasant of the day flushed, and by the time I realized that a cock pheasant was in the air I was already a day late and a dollar short.

In the willow jungle I was frustrated when Kate plunged into a thicket and four or five pheasants flushed on the other side—I could hear them, but it was too thick for me to see more than a brief glimpse of movement.

And so, another upland bird season limped to a close.

There were still two more weeks of waterfowl hunting, however, and I'd have a chance for one more hunt with Kate before her family comes back to take her home.

On our first walk of the New Year, we put up a dozen mallards. I tried for a double, but missed on my second shot. Still, there is one mallard drake down on the other side of the creek. Kate can see it and she has an urge to retrieve it, though she's hesitant to cross the creek for it. I encourage her, and she finally goes across the creek and up the opposite bank and brings the bird back to me. I praise her extravagantly.

We move on to another ranch and, at first, it looks like there aren't any ducks on the creek. Then, about 20 yards off, I spot several mallards flushing from thick weeds in the creek. I shoot and a bird drops, and Kate makes a happy retrieve. I figure these are probably the only birds in this creek, but I'm surprised when we put up another little bunch of ducks. I shoot and drop one that is just wounded. This drake mallard leads Kate on a merry chase, but she finally catches up with it and makes the retrieve. I'm surprised to see another drake mallard lying dead in the grass. I apparently made a 'Scotch double' on that rise. I send Kate after that bird and carrying the weight of three prime northern mallards, as well as knowing we have one more in the truck, I still have an extra bounce in my step.

Kate, apparently, decided, over the last couple weeks, that Grampa was okay. During this last week or so, she became my constant shadow, inside the house and out. If I moved from one room in the house to another she followed along, curling up next to my chair, ready for my next move. I guessed she was simply making the best of having been abandoned by her family, but nevertheless, it was hard to resist Katie's sweet personality.

Kate's family returned the next day, so that turned out to be Kate's last hunt of the season. It had been an interesting process, hunting with a borrowed dog. If I was unhappy and frustrated on those first few outings, I was tickled pink with our last couple trips.

With one more week of waterfowl season to go I suggested to Kevin that he could leave Kate with me, and then he could come back and get her a week later. For some reason he passed on this option.

If there's an object lesson to this story, it's that it's hard to underestimate the importance of the bond between hunter and bird dog. I've certainly heard stories of dogs that are just in it for the hunt and could care less about who might be along. I remember a long-ago magazine story about Bird Dog, the small town hunting dog of indeterminate breed. Apparently, anybody going out for a day's hunt would just stop by the owner's house and ask if Bird Dog was busy. If not, Bird Dog went along and hunted hard for anybody who would take him along.

Kate didn't transfer her loyalties that quickly. Nevertheless, once she bonded with me, she became a willing hunter and retriever.

On the morning when it was time to get in the car and go home with her family, Kate was sitting, as usual, next to my chair at the breakfast table, but keeping an anxious eye out for developments. Did she have mixed feelings about leaving to go home with her family? Maybe it's a mistake to give human feelings to animals.

Still, it seemed only right to give her a goodbye hug, just as I did to our granddaughters. Did I detect a little tear in her eye at saying goodbye, or was it just that my own eyes were a little foggy?

* * * * *

A few months later, Kate's family noted that her health seemed to be failing. Her veterinarian diagnosed Addison's Disease, an illness often associated with President John F. Kennedy, though it's also common among dogs as well. Kate hunted with Kevin a few times the next autumn, though her exercise tolerance was so limited she mostly went through the motions a short time before she was content to just walk along. She lived just a few months longer.

Our outings turned out to be her last real hunts.

Part Two

Alix – Another Great Dog

Chapter 11

Sharptails and Chokecherries

Chokecherries are ripening on the northern prairies. I look forward to picking chokecherries each year, and the rewards of chokecherry jelly on fresh biscuits, or chokecherry syrup on pancakes; great ways to get a day off to a good start.

Chokecherries mean more than filling a bucket with those fruit. It also means upland bird hunting seasons are opening, and on the prairies, early bird hunting is synonymous with hunting sharp-tailed grouse.

At one time, I considered sharptail grouse an opening act for the main attraction of pheasant hunting, but it became an addiction by itself. There's something about walking the golden grasslands of early autumn in search of sharptails. You never know what you're going to find when you go walking in search of the horizon.

The early fall prairies are full of life. Sharptails, Hungarian partridge, pheasants, mourning doves and the many songbirds that live on the prairie are there, in plenty, as the young of the year are maturing, adding their numbers to replenish the losses of the previous winter. In years when a snowy winter and plentiful rains have kept prairie potholes full of water, a stroll by a wetland may fill the air with ducks and shorebirds.

First-time visitors to the prairie often make a serious mistake when they look at the sea of grassland, stretching to the horizon, and pronounce the country as "flat." A long walk reveals rolling hills, deep coulees and draws. These draws often reveal springs and small streams. Brushy hillsides shelter deer during hot afternoons.

Then, there are the sharptails. You started the walk at dawn, taking advantage of the morning chill. Now, at mid-morning the overcast has burned off and the sun is blazing down on the grasslands. Sweat is running down your face, the salt stinging your eyes and blurring your vision. The dog is panting, looking for water. Suddenly, in a low spot in the long grasses, the dog perks up, sniffing the air, savoring the odors that, undetectable to our primitive senses, are so alluring to them. Then, with a rush of wings, birds are in the air. You raise your gun, but hesitate to shoot, thinking that the birds might be hen pheasants.

A closer look at the flushing birds, and you see that the dominant color of the birds is a spotted white, not the drab tan of a hen pheasant, and you hear the difficult-to- describe but still unmistakable "chuckle" of a sharptail as it flies. Shoot!

A bird or two falls. Reload! Hurry, because there are always stragglers. Sure enough, several more grouse get up, and another falls to the ground. Now the dog's nose really goes to work to find and retrieve the downed birds that are all but invisible in the tan grasses.

It's a long walk back, but there's a bounce to the step that was missing just a few minutes earlier, matching the bounce of birds in the back of the vest, the most uniquely satisfying feeling a bird hunter knows.

Early fall. Sharptails and chokecherries. A great time to be alive.

My introduction to sharptail grouse was in the early 1960s. We'd gotten acquainted with another couple, Chuck and Sharon, who lived in an apartment next door to where we lived. Chuck, I quickly learned, was an avid hunter and angler.

Mid-September rolled around and, with the upland bird season coming up the following weekend, Chuck suggested, "Let's go sharp-tail hunting on Saturday."

"Sure," I said. "What's a sharptail?" There are sharp-tailed grouse in Minnesota, but not in the southern areas where I grew up. I actually looked them up in an encyclopedia to learn about what we were going to be chasing the coming weekend.

We were on the road long before sunrise that Saturday, leaving the flat lands of the Red River Valley around Fargo, headed for the rolling grasslands of central North Dakota. The sun was up, but still casting long shadows when Chuck pulled off the gravel road and onto the edge of a tract of native grassland that bordered a harvested wheat field.

We got out our guns and began walking toward some distant hills. I still didn't know just what I was looking for, but suddenly birds were in the air. Shots rang out and a bird was on the ground. "Mark that bird," Chuck yelled. "They're hard to find in the grass."

He was right. A sharp-tailed grouse is almost the color of summer-cured prairie grass. Still, we found the bird and began examining our trophy. "He's got hair on his legs," Chuck pointed out. Well, maybe it was fine feathers, not hair, that covered the bird's legs and top of its feet. Chuck noted, "They're a native bird and they can take a lot more snow and cold than pheasants, because they're so well adapted to the prairie climate."

A couple years later, my friend and co-worker, Roy, and I were deer hunting in the badlands country of western North Dakota. I was walking along the top of a brushy draw and Roy was down in the bottom. I could just make out the silhouette of a sharptail grouse perched on a tree branch 100 or so yards ahead of me. "See the grouse?" Roy yelled.

"Yeah," I yelled back.

"Shoot 'im!" Roy called.

I don't claim to be a sharpshooter with a rifle, but I found a solid rest, centered the crosshairs of the 'scope on the bird's head and squeezed off a shot from my 7 x 57 Mauser. To my shock, the grouse dropped from its perch. When I walked up to retrieve the bird, I saw that I had neatly clipped off the top of its head. I don't recall whether I shot at any deer on that trip, but that grouse was the only game I brought home. Today I know that shooting at grouse with a rifle wasn't exactly legal, but I'm pretty sure that the Statute of Limitations expired long ago.

Let's fast-forward a few years and shift the scene to the shortgrass prairies of eastern Montana.

After spending several years in eastern Iowa, I was transferred to Miles City, Montana. It didn't take long to learn that the area around Miles City is some of the best hunting country in these United States.

I had many sharptail hunts in the three autumns we lived in Miles City, finding abundant grouse in the hills and prairies of the area. I'd gotten acquainted with Harley Leatherberry, a local rancher who lived by himself on his property along the Tongue River. Harley was one of those people who rarely said no to anyone or anything. Flag was a case in point. Flag was a young buck mule deer that had reportedly been orphaned the year before and bottle-fed on a neighboring ranch. When the deer got a little older, he began raiding the garden and his erstwhile foster parents ran him off. Flag ended up at Harley's. Harley didn't mind sharing his garden with Flag, and when the deer season started, brushed red paint on Flag's neck as a signal to hunters that this was a pet.

I had gotten acquainted with a couple colleagues from another government agency. Marty and Roger enjoyed hunting and fishing, so I invited them to join me for a sharptail hunt. We'd gotten Sam, our first Labrador retriever, by then.

We parked the car in Harley's yard and started walking across the wheat stubble field behind his house. Picture three hunters walking spread out in a line, across the field. In front of us, Sam was doing her thing, trying to find bird scent. Tagging along behind us was Flag. We saw cars on the road that ran past the edge of the field slam to a stop to get a better look at this strange sight.

Later, the deer got bolder and started harassing Sam, flailing out his front hooves at Sam, as if it was warding off a coyote. I had to fire a shot in the air, and finally gave the deer a swift kick in the rear end to tell him to leave my dog alone.

Some 30 years after that hunt I don't remember whether or not we got any grouse that day. I kind of recall that at the far end of the wheat field, we flushed some birds near the fenceline at the end of Harley's property, but whether we dropped any of them is one of those fuzzy facts that no longer seem important.

* * * * *

Springtime on the northern prairies is a celebration. After months of winter, the grasses are bleached a light tan and beaten down into a thick mat where the winds packed snowdrifts into low spots.

When winter loosens its hold, everything celebrates, as birds return from the south, joining the hardier inhabitants who have stayed and survived a cold, dark winter. Pheasants are strutting along the roadways, migrating geese fill the air, and ducks of all kinds fill the wetlands.

Prairie crocuses (or pasque flowers to be more exact) burst into bloom, adding their unexpected violet tones to the tan grassland. It's a celebration of light, sound, and color.

To really appreciate springtime on the prairies, however, you have to come to the prairie proms. Like the high school prom where parents and others can come and watch as their teenagers move about in unaccustomed elegance, visitors to the prairie can look in and silently marvel at a different kind of prom.

On a chilly April morning, my son, Kevin, and I stumbled across the prairie in the fading light of the full moon at 6 a.m. in search of a plywood box.

We were at North Dakota's Upper Souris National Wildlife Refuge, a 50-mile corridor of river bottom woodland, lake, and native prairie. The plywood box was a blind set out by the Refuge next to the dancing grounds of sharptail grouse. Like prairie chickens and sage grouse, sharptail grouse return every spring to a special place called a lek, where they go through springtime mating rituals.

Sharp-tailed grouse prefer a grassy hilltop for their lek, and each spring will return to the same hilltop for the spring proms.

Our blind was a mile from the road, and it was 6:30 by the time we found it. We settled in, getting out cameras and binoculars and wondering how long we would wait. It wasn't long. At 6:35, we started hearing sounds in the fading darkness, and all of a sudden there were about 10 grouse around our blind.

The grouse would split up into groups of two or three birds. Staking out sub-territories on the hilltop, they would crouch down, often flattening themselves against the ground to stare at each other. Then with wings extended, tail feathers erect, and purple air sacs inflated, they would get up and prance and twist and strut their ancient rituals, as their ancestors have done for thousands of years. Occasionally, birds would jump up and scuffle, like gamecocks, trying to establish their dominance over other male grouse. As the birds move, there are continual puffing and drumming sounds, difficult to describe, but hard to forget.

The show belongs to the male grouse. Female birds, if they are present, will hang around the margins of the ground, seemingly bored and uninterested in the dance routine. After several days, or even weeks, of dancing, the birds will mate and the females will start nesting.

People have been observing the dancing grounds for centuries, and many plains Indians developed tribal dances that reflect the rituals of the grouse. Some biologists speculate that the dancing is a means to attract predators away from any female birds. The dancing grouse are vulnerable to predators and remains of dead grouse are occasionally seen on the grounds.

The grouse seem all-absorbed in the dance, but they are still wary. Several times, the birds would suddenly all get up and fly away. Perhaps we made some unexpected noise in the blind, or they caught reflections from a camera lens. Usually they wouldn't go far and we could see them on nearby hillsides. The special hilltop had a magnetic influence and soon the birds would come walking or flying back up the hill to their dancing ground.

Other birds also took notice of the spring dance. Twice, we saw mallard drakes fly into the dancing grounds, and look in at the rituals. We could only speculate whether it was curiosity or some other urges that brought the ducks to the dance.

By mid-morning, the dance was over, and the birds had scattered to the prairie winds. The prairie wasn't silent, however. We could hear frogs croaking in the marshes, their calls competing with those of ducks and meadowlarks. Flocks of geese flew overhead, on their way to their breeding grounds in the far north.

The prairies, in April, are bursting with life, and for a few magic hours we were a part of the prairie proms.

* * * * *

My first hunt for sharptails, now over 40 years ago, didn't include a bird dog. Apartment living in cities isn't conducive to keeping dogs. We've since made up for it.

Sharp-tailed grouse marked the beginning and the beginning of the end of the career of our chocolate Labrador retriever, Alix, or Velvet Marquesa Alix, as the American Kennel Club formally knew her.

Alix was born February 10, 1985 and became part of our household on March 31 that year.

Saturday, September 14, marked the beginning of the 1985 North Dakota upland bird season, and Alix's first hunt. The season wasn't supposed to open for another week, but Governor George Sinner overruled the Game and Fish Department and opened the season early, on the basis that in North Dakota we'd better use those early fall weeks when we can. Amen.

I debated between sharp-tailed grouse and ruffed grouse for Alix's first hunt, and figured sharptails would be a better bet, as there would be a better chance of seeing birds out in open spaces—not to mention the heavier population of mosquitoes in the woodlands that could plague both of us.

It was windy and overcast, with a touch of mist in the air. Temperatures were in the mid-50s as we began our walk on a tract of long grass prairie.

We flushed our first covey of grouse within a couple hundred yards after leaving the Scout. Three got up, one at a time. I shot and missed the first two. Finally, I got the third, as it got up late. Alix didn't seem frightened by the shots but didn't quite understand what was going on.

We went over to the fallen bird and showed it to her, and gave her a chance to smell it and taste it. Hmmm, interesting!

We continued our walk and saw a grouse flush wild a long way off. Alix suddenly veered off into the wind and flushed a large covey of grouse. I shot three times—and missed every time. I reloaded and shot a single straggler. This one was just winged and Alix went over and couldn't figure this one out, as it jumped up and tried to fly. Each time it tried to jump Alix jumped back and couldn't figure what to do. She finally put her foot on it to hold it down while she pondered what to do next. Finally, she worked up her nerve to pick it up.

I muffed a couple more shooting opportunities, and we returned to the Scout for a drink and a sandwich.

After a short rest we walked some of the same cover we'd gone through earlier, and left the grass to go into a stubble field. Some other hunters were hunting the area and I was dismayed to see them flush grouse something like 25 yards from where we left the grass.

Alix was tiring now and when we walked through some tall al-falfa, she was content to walk at my heels. We finally flushed a single sharptail in short grass, which I shot and Alix retrieved, to complete our limit for the day. On the way back to the car, we walked into another covey of grouse. We were home with our birds by 1 p.m. An auspicious start to the career of a young dog.

Twelve years and a couple weeks later, Alix is a grizzled old vet-eran of a dog. Two years earlier, she had a cancerous spleen removed and made a good recovery from that surgery. This year, she developed a growth along the underside of her neck which seemed to constrict her breathing. We consulted with the veterinarian who suggested it could be surgically removed by a specialist surgeon, but it remained an unanswered question as to whether Alix could take any more radi-cal surgery, or would regain much of her old energy. We elected not to subject Alix to surgery or other radical treatment.

On an early September day, my friend John, and I took a trip to the Pintler range of southwest Montana in search of ruffed grouse in an area of aspen thickets he'd remembered from some other trip.

We found an apt looking area and began a walk into the trees. We got just a little way and Alix was wheezing and panting for air. A little further, Alix staggered and collapsed to the ground. For 10 minutes she just panted and gasped for air and I was afraid (and half hoping) that she might be done for. Finally, she recovered enough to get up and walk back to the truck. I had tears in my eyes, as we go back, and John threw an arm across my back in sympathy.

My wife had been gone for a couple days at a conference and when she came home that evening I gave her the sad news that it looked like Alix's hunting days were over and it was time to start looking for her replacement.

Nevertheless, a couple days later we left home for a weekend on the northern prairies and sharp-tailed grouse, stopping along the Missouri River to pick chokecherries along the edge of the road.

It was a warm day when we got to our campsite, so we set up camp and relaxed until early evening, when Alix and I drove to a prairie benchland overlooking the Missouri River, the scene of several sharptail hunts in prior years.

We walked through a weed patch near our parking area and Alix flushed a pheasant. By then, she was exhausted, and I led her back to the truck and tied her up next to the truck with a dish of water, while I took a long walk around the area, collecting one grouse. When I got back to the truck, just before sunset, I threw the grouse out for Alix to retrieve, which she was happy to do.

The next day, I left Alix at the trailer while I went for a hunt with my friend Jay, who came to join us for the day. He had Shadow along, a year old golden retriever pup that was about to have his first hunt. We collected four grouse in our hunt.

I got up early the next day and took Alix on a hunt in the cool of the morning. We hadn't gone too far when we walked into the middle of a covey of sharptails. I somehow managed to empty my gun twice without hitting a single bird.

I took Alix back to the truck to get a drink of water and a short rest before we took another walk. Alix picked up a fresh bird scent, flushing a single grouse. This time I did my job, dropping the bird with a single shot and giving Alix an easy retrieve. We took a slow and easy walk back to the truck, and I felt pleased that Alix had finally gotten into some birds and had a chance to make a retrieve.

That evening, just before sunset, we took another walk into the grassland, going just half an hour before Alix was totally exhausted. We turned back to the truck and at her pace, it took a full hour to get back. A thundershower was moving in and it was almost full dark by the time we got back to the truck with lightning flashing all around.

Back at camp Alix gasped and wheezed for a full two hours before she was finally able to settle down. My wife and I agreed that it looked like her hunting days were over. I was just happy that Alix got to retrieve one more bird.

It seemed a long time from just a short year earlier when we hunted that same tract of prairie. It had been a hot day, but by 6 p.m. it had cooled to 70° with a cool wind blowing.

We walked into the grassland and I spotted a pair of grouse flying far ahead over a big coulee, landing in a grassy area on the other side of the draw. I figured we didn't have many better options, so we took a long walk to the edge of the prairie, across a wheat stubble field, down one side of the coulee and up the other. We finally got to the grassy area where we saw the birds land. Walking toward the edge of the coulee a sharptail flushed. I swung on the bird and hit it with my first shot. The bird went down hard on the edge of the coulee and actually bounced a foot into the air. Alix found the bird about 20 vertical feet below where it had bounced.

The sun was setting as we walked back to the truck. A lone cottonwood tree marked the edge of an old farmstead, outlined in gold against the sky.

Author's note: This wasn't the end of Alix's career, though it was the beginning of the end. Her late hunts and last days are detailed in the final chapter, "Transitions."

Chapter 12

The ESPN Hunt

A special place—the Rocky Mountain Front country of Montana where the prairie meets the mountains. It's vast, rimmed on the west by a wall of mountains. The mountains set a boundary to the plains, but the influence of the mountains also create wild variations in weather that make life on the plains interesting.

This is Chinook Country, where winds spilling over the mountains onto the plains can either freeze the country solid, or can melt deep snow and send temperatures soaring in another few hours.

It's a three-hour drive, this November morning, to the Rocky Mountain Front. It's cool and sunny at home, but I run into snow showers on the prairies. Friends are expecting me, and heavy snow is falling when I arrive at their home. Temperatures are mild—in the mid-30s—but the snow is wet and heavy. It's snowing so hard that hunting seems impossible. By mid-afternoon, however, the snow has let up and I head out for a late afternoon hunt.

At 3:30 p.m. it is snowing, again, with temperatures dropping. The farmstead has a patch of trees and brush adjoining the edge of grain stubble. We're walking the edge of the trees when Alix, my chocolate Labrador retriever, picks up a scent and flushes a pheasant rooster at long range. It's a long shot, but I swing on it and the bird pauses its wingbeats for just a fraction of a second, then resumes flying, strong and fast. Suddenly, it collapses and hits the ground in a cloud of powdery snow.

After collecting the bird we resume walking the perimeter of the field but see nothing until we come to a weed patch where an irrigation ditch crosses the fenceline marking the farm's property line. Alix picks up a scent and follows it to a clump of tall weeds. She has this way of pinning down pheasants and then willing them to fly. I suppose some pointing Lab enthusiasts would say she was pointing. Perhaps, but I won't get into that. This bird didn't want to budge and Alix finally pounced on it, springing a cock pheasant into the air. I shoot, dropping the bird. It is lightly hit, however, and hits the ground running, seeking shelter in a weedy ditch that parallels the fenceline. Alix was up to the challenge. She picks up the scent, goes into the ditch and retrieves the bird. Two pheasants in the bag.

This farm has a cattail slough in one corner and it can be a hotspot. It's also right across the road from another farm, however, and a black Lab from this farm suddenly joins us. I have a momentary thought that with two bird dogs, I should have some hot shooting. I think otherwise when the blackie runs wild in the cover, flushing pheasants all over, all out of range. I finally succeed in sending her home. By this time, however, there are only a few hens left.

It reminded me of another hunt in a previous season, just a few miles away, when the farmer's white dog ran along with us as we drove from the farmstead to the CRP field we were going to hunt. While my companion, Glenn, and I watched helplessly, that white dog bounded through the field, flushing pheasants everywhere. By the time she was done, she'd flushed scores of birds from the field. We wanted to shoot that blasted mutt, but didn't think that was any way to stay in the landowner's good graces.

The slough corner now devoid of pheasants, Alix and I started working the irrigation ditches back to where we started. We flushed another rooster in some long grass where two ditches merge. I dropped this one with my first shot and anchored it with a second. It's now 5:10 p.m. and it's dark by the time I get back to the truck, but Alix and I have a three-bird limit in just an hour and a half of hunting.

This whole hunt seems like a miracle. Six months earlier, Alix's life hung in the balance. She suddenly wasn't able to hold food down and acted sick. Our veterinarian took x-rays and could see a mass in her abdomen and did surgery. Alix had a cancer of the spleen and the tumor had consumed it. Following a splenectomy, Alix made a quick recovery and by fall, a grizzled 10-year-old veteran and a cancer survivor, she was eager to hunt.

The next morning, my friend, Jay Pottenger, joined me for breakfast at the local café before our hunt. Jay had put down Caesar, his big yellow Lab, the previous spring when he was diagnosed with untreatable cancer, so he was anxious to hunt.

Overnight, the skies have cleared and it is bitter cold. It is clear and sunny, but the temperatures will remain below zero all day.

The countryside is white with a foot of snow from yesterday's storm. We start at a farm that has been one of Jay's favorite spots. The fields look like a scene from the Arctic. It's solid white and not a sign of wildlife anywhere. Crossing the deep snow of a low spot, however, Alix acts like there is a scent in a clump of snow-covered grass. Alix jumps on it and a cock pheasant springs out. I swing and shoot, dropping the pheasant cleanly. There were no tracks anywhere, so this is where the bird spent the night while snows piled up around him.

We move to another farm that is situated on a hillside, with creeks and irrigation ditches cutting through the middle of it. There are grassy areas between fencelines and ditches that haven't been mowed or grazed. Pheasant heaven.

We see tracks in the snow where the ditches border wheat stubble, and Jay gets a rooster right away. A little later, another pheasant gets up and I shoot. The bird keeps flying, although I see a leg drop. "Darn," I think, "a lost bird," as it disappears in the distance.

We resume the hunt and from a brush patch, pheasants are flushing, well out of range. In one brush clump, Alix flushes a covey of Hungarian partridge and I am able to drop one of the speedsters. Alix makes a quick retrieve.

Further down the hillside, Alix picks up another scent and tries to flush the bird. It's holding tight, and won't flush. Finally, Alix sticks her head into the snow and comes up with a pheasant. The bird is very much alive, but has a broken leg, so we've recovered my bird of 15 minutes earlier.

At the bottom of the hillside, there is a pasture with light, marshy cover. Alix is working ahead of us and flushes a cock pheasant and I take a long quartering-away shot at it and the bird drops like a stone. Jay teases me, "Vang, you're just unconscious today." What can I say? My 20 gauge Ruger over/under is a heckuva bird-getter.

At 1:10 p.m. Jay collected our sixth pheasant for the day's limit.

That night, at bedtime, it has dipped to 25° below zero, with stars sparkling coldly in the clear sky. I'm not worried about birds spoiling in the ice chest in the back of the truck, but do worry about whether the truck will start in the morning.

Morning comes and I gird against the elements. Hunting in sub-zero conditions is quite feasible. The trick is having enough layers, so you can peel a layer or two, or open up to let off steam. So, long underwear, wool shirt, vest, coat, in addition to brush pants and boots is the uniform for the day.

Feeling adequately bundled, I step outside the motel room. To my surprise, it's warm outside. During the night, a Chinook blew in, and temperatures are in the 30s. Water is dripping off the roof and the snow is turning to slush. I hastily shed most of those layers before meeting Jay for breakfast.

We return to Pheasant Heaven, with plans to hit a couple other farms later, if necessary.

The pheasants are still there. Jay picks up one cock within 100 yards from where we parked the truck. Moving on, we both shoot at a flushing pheasant. The bird drops, but lands on his feet at a dead run. We're afraid we might lose that bird, but Alix picks up the scent in grassy cover and makes the retrieve.

At the crest of the hill, we each flush pheasants and make our shots. The retrieves are easy and we have four birds in the bag.

Alix then picks up scent in a patch of standing barley and follows it until the bird flushes, giving Jay an easy shot and an easy retrieve.

In tall grass, Alix picks up another scent and follows it to a clump of weeds. She knows there's a bird in there, but it holds tight until she lunges, and another rooster pheasant comes out, clawing for air. I make the shot, and at 9:55 a.m. we have our sixth and final bird of the day.

We have a relaxed stroll back to the truck, enjoying gentle, warm breezes, which have reduced yesterday's knee-deep snow to slushy patches, as well as the pleasant heft of limits of pheasants in the back of our vests. We hope to flush some partridge along the way, but are disappointed. Alix keeps looking for pheasants, however, and flushes a pair just 10 yards from where I'd parked my truck.

It has been quite an outing. In three days of hunting, we've taken 15 pheasant roosters with one bonus partridge. Alix showed the benefits of experience, as she again and again flushed tight-holding pheasants without losing a single bird that we knocked down. I wish, often, that someone could have been along for the hunt with a video camera filming us as Alix followed scents to holding birds and making one retrieve after another.

As Jay said, on our stroll back to the truck, "We had a pheasant hunt that could have been on ESPN."

A footnote to the ESPN hunt is that this turned out to be our last hunt on the hillside farm. The owner was having financial problems and sold it. The following year there was new fencing all around the property and NO TRESPASSING signs everywhere. We'd had several good hunts on the farm and have great memories, but it hurts when I think that I'll never again hunt this little piece of pheasant paradise.

Part Three

Essays and Stories

Chapter 13

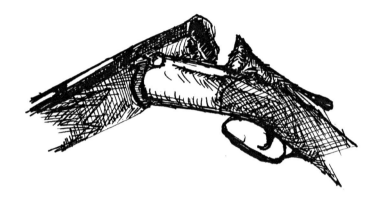

The Annual Report

The room is quiet. The chairman is fussing with his notes and refers to an instruction booklet. He had conducted many annual meetings over the years, but was nervous about this one.

In the back of the room, the chief executive officer has a thinly disguised look of impatience on her face. Her right hand unconsciously drops down to scratch the ears of the stockholder, a dignified looking Labrador retriever. The CEO whispers to the stockholder, "Honestly, I don't know why he can't simply give us a written report, instead of going through this routine." The stockholder rolls over on his back and nuzzles the CEO's hand. If the stockholder shared the CEO's impatience, he didn't seem overly disturbed.

Finally, the chairman cleared his throat and announces, "I hereby call this annual meeting to order." Continuing, he says, "The Year 2000 has been a positive year." He tapped several keys on a laptop computer, and a PowerPoint slide was projected on a screen behind the chairman. "You will notice," the chairman continued, "we have taken steps to further improve the presentation of the annual report, by using the latest presentation software and hardware, instead of an overhead projector."

The CEO whispers to the stockholder, "He means he got some new toys. I hope he learned how to use them."

The chairman ignores the disruption and taps another computer key, bringing up a bar chart on the screen. "You will note from this chart that we made 12 outings in search of ruffed grouse." With his laser pointer, he pointed to a second bar, saying, "This establishes that during this past grouse season we averaged 6.5 productive flushes per day, which represents a significant improvement over fiscal 1999, when there was an average of 5.2 flushes per day."

The CEO breaks in to ask, "There seems to be something missing here. If you went grouse hunting 12 times, and averaged 6.5 productive flushes per day; that means you had shots at 78 grouse. I remember having grouse for dinner only three times. Can you explain this discrepancy?"

The chairman's face reddened. "I was coming to that," he said. "This next chart," he said, tapping a key, "shows my analysis of our performance in this area. Of 78 grouse flushed, 20 disappeared into the trees before I had a chance to shoot. Thus, of the remaining 58 grouse flushed, I fired a total of 75 shots. I can confirm that aspen trees got in the way of 14 of those shots. I actually harvested five grouse, and the remaining 56 shots apparently did not hit anything."

"Now, you may consider our performance lacking in this area," the chairman continued. "However, you may remember that the understory brush in the coverts was unusually heavy this year. My successful harvesting of five grouse indicates a positive success rate of 6.7 percent, which is actually an improvement over our last fiscal year." He concluded by noting, "There are in fact a brace of grouse still in the freezer which I'm saving for a special occasion. There will be an interdepartmental memo to notify you in ample time to clear your calendar for this event."

The CEO grumbled, but acknowledging a deep appreciation for ruffed grouse dinners, she merely tells the chairman, "Please continue."

"Yes, thank you," the chairman says. "At this time, I would like to commend our retrieving division for outstanding performance." The stockholder wagged happily, as the CEO began scratching a particularly sensitive spot at the base of his tail. "This chart indicates that, of 29 retrieving opportunities, the retrieving division successfully completed 29 retrieves. In addition," he noted, "on two different occasions, he tracked down and retrieved crippled pheasants that other hunters had missed. Thus, the retrieving division had an actual success rate of 107 percent."

At this news, there was a standing ovation for the stockholder. The stockholder acknowledged the ovation with his normally modest demeanor, wagging his tail, though he did break decorum a bit when he jumped up to give the CEO an enthusiastic kiss.

The chairman taps his gavel to bring the meeting back to order. "There is more to our report than shooting and retrieving," he announces. "In our flyfishing department, I am happy to report 45 separate outings in the core performance area of March through September."

"I had noticed you were gone a lot," commented the CEO. "Now, would you mind explaining your absence of 52 days, when you report only 45 days of fishing?"

"There was some travel involved," the Chairman acknowledged. "For example, two full days of travel are needed to get to Patagonia. The round trip alone accounts for four days." He clarified the point further, "While I was returning from Patagonia, it seemed logical to make a two day stopover in Belize on the way back. The bonefishing was at a seasonal peak, and the stopover was quite an economical way to sample the opportunities."

The CEO groans at the chairman's alleged economies, and pointed out, "I don't recall anything scheduled in the budget for international travel. Would you explain that item further?"

The Chairman reached into his notes for a handout and pointed out a large budgeted item for 'unexpected contingencies,' and said, "I'm well aware you may have had some other possible plans in this area. I'm sure, however, you will confirm there was nothing more unexpected than my fishing trip to Patagonia. Thus this is well contained in this budget item."

Sensing hostility in the air, the chairman taps a key, and announces, "Moving right along, I think it's time to present the budget for the coming fiscal year." With his laser pointer, he highlights several items. "There have been some concerns expressed about my shooting performance. Therefore, the budget shows a line item for a season's membership at the Old Hickory Sporting Clays Club. Another line item will detail a modest increase in the amounts budgeted for shotgun shells."

The CEO is rising to her feet to make an objection. The chairman quickly moves on to the next line item. "I know how concerned you are about my shooting. Thus, the next item will seem logical. I have a lead on a matched pair of Purdey shotguns at a most reasonable…"

The graphic on the screen suddenly went blank and a new message appeared. "Fatal Error. Your program will be shut down."

The CEO laughed hilariously and exclaimed, "I couldn't agree more. I move the meeting be adjourned."

The CEO stands and leaves the room in search of a fresh drink and a rawhide chewbone for the stockholder. The chairman stands at the podium for a few moments, then picks up his notes and turns off the computer.

"Yes, well that went rather well, don't you think?" he says to an apparently empty room.

The stockholder stands up, stretches, yawns, and trots off for his chewbone.

Chapter 14

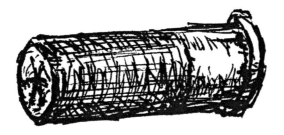

Hunting and Killing

It's September and hunting seasons have started. From now until mid-January, much of my outdoors time will be spent with a shotgun or rifle in hand, and some of the season's experiences often end up in print.

In short, I write about hunting and hunting will, sooner or later, deal with the death of an animal. It's sometimes an awkward topic about which to write. It's sometimes difficult to read about. In fact, a month ago, one local resident mentioned to my wife, "I usually don't read your husband's newspaper column. I don't like the killing."

I was surprised at the comment. While I often write about hunting, I don't often dwell on the death of the animal I'm hunting. It's easier and probably more pleasant to write about fall colors, north winds, and all the other sights and sounds of the outdoors.

The arena of the hunt is, literally, as big as all outdoors and I like to think of that arena as my usual topic. So, I write about the antics of my dog, or geese flying high overhead, and the sight of golden aspens against snowcapped-mountains. If we're honest about hunting, we have to admit that we spend more time looking at scenery than we do stalking prey.

Yet, if we're honest about hunting, we also have to acknowledge that killing is an integral part of the hunt. First of all, we hunt for food. At the end of the season, I don't have to look any farther than my freezer shelves to determine whether I had a successful season. We eat game throughout the year and the luxury of having pheasant dinners in August depends on my having shot pheasants the previous season. I'm not addicted to elk hunting (I'd rather follow my dog across a field or duck marsh) but I like having a freezer full of elk meat.

Our nation's population has doubled during my lifetime. The average U. S. citizen is now a city-dweller, and has never spent time on a farm or a ranch. Most American have never fed a steer or hog, knowing that their family's economic survival depends on sending that animal to a slaughterhouse. A chicken dinner, for many, means a stop at a fast food franchise. When I was a kid, chicken dinner meant someone (often that was me) caught an old hen and whacked off its head with an axe.

There are factions in our society that assert that sport hunting is wrong. Many people in these factions are sincere in their beliefs. There are many agendas in their protests. Some people protest opening dove hunting in states that haven't previously had dove seasons. Others protest the culling of excess bison in the Yellowstone National Park area. In some states they've managed to outlaw mountain lion hunting, or bear hunting.

The ultimate goal of these so-called "animal rights" organizations is to put an end to all hunting, and that's just a start. Fishing is next on their agenda. If you're a fly angler and generally practice 'catch and release,' don't think you're exempt. As far as the animal rights organizations are concerned, we're just torturing fish for our own pleasure.

Sincerity in one's beliefs, however, does not make a person right. In my opinion, a fundamental dishonesty exists in thinking that we can go through life without causing the death of animals. If we eat meat and wear leather we are direct beneficiaries of an animal's death. Even a vegan, a strict vegetarian who eats no meats or dairy products and even avoids wearing leather, can't go through life without impacting animal's lives.

The truth is that as we go through life we cause death. We have options, however. We can buy groceries at the store and pretend that food is an industrial product—which seems increasingly true when we read the list of chemicals on package labels.

I find satisfaction in being a participant. Thus, I hunt. Though by Nature's standards I'm an inefficient predator, my nature hikes sometimes result in my shooting at an animal. If I do my job, the animal dies quickly and is brought to possession.

At the same time, however, I confess that when I occasionally catch one of those hunting shows on TV, I'm sometimes a little queasy when the shows make a special thing about showing "impact shots." In fact, I was downright upset by a DVD I once saw that had a whole segment of nothing but impact shots. As far as I was concerned, this video was disrespectful of wildlife. A Native American traditionally apologized to the animal after bringing it down. In some European traditions, a successful hunter puts a sprig of a pine branch in the deer's mouth, symbolizing a final bite of food. I can't think of anything more opposite to this ancient tradition than a video showing nothing but impact shots—even if I couldn't avoid a morbid fascination with the program.

I care for my game as best I can and store it properly. Later, I prepare game for the table and, with a prayer of thanks, we celebrate the festive meal and recall the days afield that made it possible.

Hunting does cause death, but it's an essential part of my life.

Note: The original version of this essay was published in our local newspaper on September 13, 2001, two days after the September 11 terrorist attacks. I was able to include the following addendum: "Dear Readers: The above thoughts about hunting were written and submitted prior to the tragic events of Tuesday. Like most of you, I am overwhelmed with shock and grief. I apologize if any readers are offended by the timing of this discussion of hunting and the associated deaths of animals during the hunt. If anything, however, this attack on our country underlines the fact that our hikes up a mountainside or across a prairie in search of food and recreation are innocent compared to the evil people inflict on their fellow humans. God bless America."

Chapter 15

Trophies

When we think about trophies, we usually think antlers or horns. I do, In fact, have a mounted white-tailed deer head in our family room, a souvenir of the 1983 opening day of the North Dakota deer season. At the season-opening stroke of 12 Noon, a big buck, with heavy antlers and swollen neck, walked in front of me. I mean, right in front of me. He wasn't more than 20 feet away.

I blinked, and even glanced down at my watch to see if shooting time had arrived. It had. I raised my rifle and shot. The deer made a leap and started running, and I thought, "I'd better take another shot." Then, I reconsidered, "No way I missed that one." The deer went about 20 yards and collapsed in mid-leap, his antlers hanging up in a small tree.

I dressed it out, tagged it and walked back to my Scout and drove to the farmhouse to tell my farmer host of my luck. Joe, a veteran of many deer hunts over his 70+ years, volunteered to help me load the deer. When we got in the woods, he looked at my buck, slapped me on the back and said, "That's the trophy of a lifetime, boy."

Grinning ear to ear, it didn't take me long to drive back to town. After a couple stops to show it off, I was home and on the phone calling Jon, the son of a neighbor and a part-time taxidermist. Several months later, his work was done and my trophy was hanging on the wall.

I'm proud of this trophy deer. While it's more a souvenir of dumb luck than hunting skill, it reminds me, again, of that day, and many more. It also reminds me of days I never fired a shot, yet had experiences that are vivid in my mind even though there were no tangible mementos of the day.

On another wall hangs a pheasant, forever frozen in flight by Jon's taxidermy skills.

It was a mid-October day in the late 1970s. Kevin, then a teenager, had a few days off from school for teacher's convention—our annual opportunity for a father-son pheasant hunt.

We were hunting in south central North Dakota, not far from the South Dakota line. We had walked several areas that day, and had probably picked up a pheasant or two.

We were feeling discouraged. Pheasants had come back from their collapse in the mid '60s, but it was nothing like what I had experienced back in the old Soil Bank days. Along a dusty back road, however, we saw a harvested cornfield with shelterbelts on three sides of the field. It looked promising.

We parked at a pullout and started walking. In a cornrow, not far from the shelterbelt that ran along the long side of the field, a pheasant flushed from just behind me, and rocketed off for safety. I whirled around and shot, but to no apparent effect. The bird kept flying hard and strong, out of range for follow-up shots.

"Drat!" I thought. "That was a beautiful bird." But missing an occasional shot is just as much a part of pheasant hunting as walking. We continued to work the corn stubble, and started going up the shelterbelt on the east end of the field. In the corner where the two rows of trees met, Kevin suddenly called, "Hey, Dad, look at this," holding in his hands a large and very dead pheasant.

We studied the bird for a few moments. It was a big pheasant, fully feathered and not a mark on it. It was still warm and limp.

At the time we thought it was likely a bird, lightly hit by some hunter, that flew away only to die in this patch of brush. One thing was clear. This pheasant was too beautiful to just pluck and put in the freezer for a future dinner. We carefully carried it back to the car and when we got home the next day we took it to Jon.

Several months later, the pheasant took his place of honor on the wall. Over the years, many guests have admired the bird, and shared hunting memories of their own, triggered by seeing my pheasant.

I have relived that hunt many times and I again see the pheasant that flushed from that cornfield flying away, seemingly unscathed by my hurried shot. Then I think of Kevin finding the pheasant in the trees. A hunter who didn't shoot well enough to anchor the bird lost that beautiful North Dakota pheasant. The hunter who couldn't shoot was, without doubt, me.

That pheasant is a large, handsome specimen of a Chinese ring-necked pheasant. If you measure a pheasant by its tailfeathers, however, it isn't my best bird-hunting trophy.

In November 1972, I escaped the house on a Sunday afternoon for a few hours of pheasant hunting on Harley's ranch along the Tongue River, in southeastern Montana.

In a corner formed where several fields came together, there was a patch of brush and trees that often produced pheasants.

I walked into the brush, and my two year old black Lab, Sam, flushed a pheasant. With a hurried shot through the trees, more typical of ruffed grouse shooting, I dropped the pheasant. Sam had trouble finding the bird, and I finally found it myself, lying on some short grass in the middle of the patch. Like my North Dakota bird it was virtually unmarked. Unlike my future trophy, however, it had long, long tailfeathers, and long spurs on its feet. This old bird was a survivor, or at least it had been until this gray November afternoon.

I had long wanted a mounted pheasant, but at this time in our lives, food in the freezer seemed more important than spending money on taxidermy services.

Over the years, I have regretted this decision many times. While my later North Dakota pheasant is beautiful, its tail feathers measure a mere 18 inches. The tail feathers of that Montana bird, which I still have, stretch out to a seemingly impossible 26 inches.

I have taken other long-tailed cockbirds over the years, and I have preserved many of those tail feathers. There have been some impressive birds, but none had tail feathers that seriously challenge 26 inches.

One feather, the souvenir of an overcast November day that turned into a roaring northern Montana prairie blizzard, reminds me of Alix, my chocolate Lab, who flushed and retrieved the bird. This pheasant had feathers that, worn by its daily walks through brush and thorns, tapered to the slenderest of widths the last of its 23 inches.

The day before Thanksgiving, last fall, I was desperate for a good pheasant hunt. I had spent many days hunting deer and had nothing to show for it but frustration. I needed success, so Candy and I hit the road for prairie country. Candy picked up a scent and locked on to a bird holding in wheat stubble along a fenceline. The bird flushed. I swung, pulled the trigger, and the bird dropped. I felt like a weight had been lifted from my shoulders—the slump was broken. When Candy retrieved the bird I thought, "Wow, look at the length of his tail." This bird was another old survivor who had run out of luck. He had long tailfeathers, but they came to only 24 inches.

Every trophy has a story, as the trophy usually represents more than long feathers or heavy antlers.

In the 1980s, I visited the Winnipeg, Manitoba office of an executive with Canada's Social Insurance System. Our business completed, I noted a mounted cock pheasant that graced the office wall. "That's a nice looking pheasant," I said.

"That's a souvenir of my last day in Alberta," he said. His previous job had been in Calgary. He had gotten a promotion and the moving van was coming. His next-door neighbor called him at 7 a.m. and suggested, "Let's go out and get one more pheasant before you leave."

"Sorry, I can't go. I've got movers coming at 9:00."

"Heck, we'll be back by 9:00."

"Well, I was back at 9:00 all right," he recalled with a sheepish grin. "But, it was 9 p.m. The movers had come and gone, and my wife wasn't speaking to me."

Taxidermy preserves memories in a three-dimensional way that photographs and paintings can only begin to suggest. The pheasant on my wall is the touchstone of many birds, many hunts, and most of all, the Labrador retrievers that always made our hunts memorable.

I will always regret, however, not having spent the money to mount that Tongue River pheasant with his 26-inch tail feathers. Whatever it might have cost to have a pheasant mounted in 1972 would have been forgotten many years ago, but I still remember, on the dinner table, that old bird was tough as shoe leather.

Chapter 16

Rough Shooting – American Style

I believe it was Winston Churchill who once described the United States and England as "Two great peoples separated by a common language."

An example of how Americans and the English use their language differently is in describing outdoor activities.

Here in the United States, if we tell our neighbors, "I'm going hunting tomorrow," they would understand that we're going to get out a rifle or shotgun, or archery equipment, perhaps, and go off in search of game. If all goes well, we might come home with a duck or pheasant, or a deer or elk. There are almost endless possibilities.

On the other hand, if we lived in the U.K. and announced to our neighbours (there's another difference in our common tongues), "We're going hunting," they'd have a different understanding. They would assume we were going to saddle the horses and go riding off behind a pack of hounds in search of a fox.

If, back in the U.K., we took the shotgun in search of ducks or pheasants, we would say we were "going shooting." Taking this a step further, we need to define whether it's a shoot where we paid an estate owner a pile of money to participate in a "driven shoot," or were going to take the dog and walk the uplands or hedgerows in search of game. In a driven shoot, there would be a crew of people walking the brush and hillsides flushing pheasants or other game birds and chasing them toward the shooters.

Just going for a walk to find game would be called "rough shooting."

Finally, if you were in search of deer in the British Isles, you would be "stalking." If you were in search of an antlered deer, such as the red deer of Scotland, which is similar to our American elk or wapiti, you would be stalking a stag.

What seems to lack definition in our American version of the sporting language is the outing where there is no shooting, although it seems rough at times, and about all that happens is a lot of driving.

Much of the English sporting terminology revolves around the fact that, in the British Isles, wildlife belongs to the landowner. On most estates, pheasants or grouse are a valuable crop that, in reality, gets harvested twice. First of all, wealthy shotgunners pay serious money to landowners for the opportunity to shoot game, and for the piles of pounds they pay, they bloody well expect do a lot of shooting. They may, over the course of a weekend, shoot hundreds of birds, but will likely go home with only a "brace" or two as a souvenir of the weekend. The landowner ships the bulk of the birds to city markets where game-hungry shoppers buy wildfowl for gourmet dinners.

It's a heckuva deal. It's kind of like a North Dakota wheat farmer getting custom combine operators to come in and harvest the farmer's crop and then pay the farmer for the privilege.

Things are changing in the United States, with shooting preserves popping up in many areas around the countryside. Some even offer English style 'driven' pheasant shoots. I'm not ready to say this is good or bad. In any event, preserve hunting offers some new alternatives to train dogs or get in some bird hunting (in the American sense) in the off season.

Still, for me the real essence of upland hunting and waterfowling is the opportunity to go out with my dog and shotgun in search of whatever adventure we might find. Sometimes, using English terminology to create confusion, we often go shooting, but there's the good chance we'll come home from a shoot without firing a shot.

Last January, for example, my hunting partner and I went out after ducks in the closing days of the Montana waterfowl season. We saw more whitetail deer in the river bottoms than we ever saw in November. We saw pheasants along the roadside. Apparently aware that the pheasant season was closed, the roosters just cackled their scorn at us. A herd of pronghorn antelope was bedded down in a patch of sagebrush, enjoying mild winter weather.

We did see ducks. However, they saw us first and scattered for parts unknown. We put out decoys and took cover, awaiting their return, or for new flights that might want to take a rest with their Styrofoam cousins. Hours later, shivering in spite of relatively mild weather, we pulled the dekes and warmed ourselves with sandwiches and coffee. Adding insult to injury, several flights of Canada geese passed overhead, just out of range, while we ate.

I'm not alone in these shootless shoots. Frustration is part of the game. A friend told of taking several waterfowling trips, coming home empty-handed. He turned down a chance to go duck and goose hunting, one weekend, and, instead, went ice fishing at an area lake. What did he get? One small trout. His partner went hunting, and came home with several geese and a limit of mallards.

I've been keeping a hunting diary since 1985 and wish I had started sooner. I frequently go back into my scribbled entries, and relive outings I've had, some alone and others with partners. Some of those partners, human and canine, are now among the departed, though their memories are preserved in my diary entries. My diary holds many memories; days of golden aspens and blue skies, a dog's first grouse, pheasants in a snowstorm. Many days, however, more than I like to admit, I summed up, simply, as, "A long walk."

One of those walks, last September, was frustrating. The weekend started in a bad way, when we had a breakdown on our camping trailer, which meant spending much of my hunting time running to RV dealers in a strange city looking for parts. The trailer finally repaired, I went out before sunset in search of sharptail grouse.

I made a long circle around a large tract of BLM grassland. Candy flushed several pheasants from a dried-up slough at the beginning of the walk. Unfortunately, pheasant season was still a couple weeks off. We spotted one sharp-tailed grouse that flushed way out of range and headed for the horizon. With just minutes of legal shooting time left before dark, Candy flushed a pair of pheasants. Then she flushed another. I didn't shoot, of course, but as this last bird disappeared into distance, it occurred to me that the bird didn't have a long tail, and then I heard a telltale "chuckle." "Expletive deleted," I thought. "That was a sharptail, and I just watched it go."

That's the way it goes. About the only guarantee we have when we go out in search of game is that we'll get plenty of fresh air. As to those days when we come home empty-handed, we often say, in terms that would make absolutely no sense in England, "That's why we call it hunting, and not shooting."

Chapter 17

A New Place to Hunt

There was a sense of excitement and, perhaps, nervousness, as I drove into the ranch. I wondered what I would find.

A year earlier, at a Trout Unlimited program, a fellow angler mentioned, "You should get acquainted with Jim Adams (that's not his true name, let me point out). He has a ranch on No Name Creek, and he's mentioned that he has pheasants."

I made a note of Jim's name and phone number, though I confess that when the pheasant season ended a month later I hadn't made that call.

I was at another TU meeting the following spring and my friend asked, "Remember my rancher friend I was telling you about? He's over there," he said, "Let me introduce you."

We had a cordial conversation and Jim said I'd be welcome to come and hunt on his ranch in the fall.

It was mid-November and I'd made a couple weekend trips for pheasants. With winter setting in it was time to concentrate on local hunts, and after playing phone tag, I finally connected with Jim, getting directions to his ranch.

Jim was doing some work in his ranch shop when I got there in mid-morning. A bull elk his son, a senior at the state university, had shot the previous weekend was hanging and aging. Jim put his work aside to show me the layout of the ranch property, suggested where I could park my truck, and then left me to my own devices.

A creek wanders through the property at the base of the hillside below the ranch buildings. I could see patches of willows and cattail sloughs in the bottoms. If there were pheasants around, this is where they'd be.

Candy and I walked down the hillside to the creek bottom. I quickly decided it was a good thing I hadn't come here earlier in the season, as the marshy bottoms are easier to walk after the water is frozen. We hadn't gotten far into the cover before pheasants began flushing wild. Jim said only one person had hunted birds here since the season opened a month earlier, but that certainly didn't mean that the pheasants were naïve, and that certainly was the case that morning.

As we explored our way through the willows, a pheasant flushed, presenting a difficult but makeable shot before it disappeared. Unfortunately, I missed. As we continued our walk more pheasants flushed, but it seemed like they kept getting up on the wrong side of the trees, flying off unseen, or just giving me a glimpse, or getting up into the sun, so I couldn't pick out the colors of a rooster.

We also pushed out several whitetail deer, including a nice buck. I had my rifle and an un-punched deer tag along, but Jim said his daughter thinks the deer are her pets, so there was no deer hunting in the creek bottoms.

I'd made a long circle, back to just down the hillside from where I'd parked the truck, when a flushing cock pheasant startled me. I got a shot off at the bird, but missed and he was out of range for a second shot.

We're close enough to the truck to declare a sandwich break and, enjoying some mild November sunshine after early morning temperatures near zero, I reflected on my good fortune to be here and seeing pheasants, even if I hadn't brought any birds down in our first walk.

Starting from scratch 15 years earlier, I've managed to accumulate some good hunting spots in the area. Some have been the result of introductions, such as on this hunt, some are on public land, and then there have been a few I've just luckily blundered into.

It was the fall of 1988 when I went exploring on some back roads on a Veteran's Day weekend. I hoped to find a place to hunt in what was still unfamiliar territory to me. I debated packing the rifle or shotgun, and much to the delight of Alix, my chocolate Lab, I chose the shotgun. At the least, I hoped to find a farmer or rancher who might sell me a bale of straw to put in Alix's doghouse for winter warmth.

I stopped at one farm, looking for straw, and the lady there suggested I might try the Jefferson ranch (again, a fictitious name) just down the road, where, "Maybe; they had some grain."

I found the ranch where I was greeted by a whole pack of dogs and a distinguished-looking older gentleman. He said, "Well, I put up 450 bales of straw this summer, but the cows got into the stack and scattered the whole works." Then, apparently seeing some disappointment cross my face, added, "Did you want to hunt?"

I allowed as how I might. We went into the house where his wife gave me a permission slip.

I drove through a set of gates to get away from the yard and followed a dirt trail into the pastures, not expecting much. Ray, the rancher, said there were a few deer around, and maybe some ducks in the sloughs.

We were barely out of the yard when a couple deer came bouncing out of a patch of brush. A little further a couple more ran off. At the end of the trail, I parked the Scout by a partially frozen slough and Alix and I began to explore possibilities.

We walked along the slough, flushing a couple hen mallards. I watched them fly off, unscathed. Then, Alix plunged into a patch of trees and brush. I barely had time to react to her change of direction when I heard the sound of a cock pheasant flushing with a flurry of scolds. With that jolt to my system, I followed Alix into the brush. Several more pheasants flushed. I got a shot at one and missed and then thought some unprintable words when my pump gun jammed, preventing me from getting a second shot off at the bird.

A few minutes later I had another unsuccessful shot at a pheasant. Later that afternoon I had some shots at ducks, concluding the day's action.

Before heading for home I sat on the tailgate of the Scout and reflected on a marvelous day. Maybe I was going home with an empty game bag, but I found hospitable ranch hosts as well as game all over the place. I enjoyed pleasant afternoon sunshine while snow showers hung over the mountains just west of the river bottoms we were hunting.

A week later, I went out for an early Saturday morning deer hunt with Frank, a colleague from the office. I got home after a morning of following deer tracks through a canyon, but without seeing any deer. After I finished reading the paper and mail, my wife said, "Why don't you take Alix hunting, so we can stand her."

We returned to the Jefferson ranch and in a wandering walk, we flushed a pair of mallard drakes from a slough and I managed to drop one of them in the water. Alix swam out to get it, but took it to the bank on the other side and played with it while I stood and screamed imprecations at her. She finally brought the duck back and we resumed our hunt. In a clump of brush, Alix rousted out a tight-sitting pheasant. I dropped it on the second shot. It landed running, but Alix was Johnny on the spot and caught it before it could make a getaway.

With the combined heft of a drake mallard and cock pheasant in the back of my vest, there was a new bounce in my stride as I thought to myself, "Deer, elk, ducks, pheasants, and ruffed grouse, all within an hour's drive of home. All that, and trout streams, too. Maybe this area isn't paradise, but it'll do."

Over two hunting seasons, this ranch became almost a home away from home. I took a nice forkhorn whitetail buck on the ranch in that first season, as well as more pheasants and ducks. Several times I was startled when I approached the river along the edge of the property and put up flocks of Canadian geese that had been resting along the shoreline. I was really surprised, one other afternoon, when a ruffed grouse flushed from a riparian jungle, appearing for just an instant—long enough for me to identify it, but not enough time to swing my gun at it.

My last hunt on the ranch closed the 1989 upland season. Alix and I were walking along a fenceline next to a stubble field. Alix flushed a cock pheasant from the fenceline cover that flew directly toward me. I waited until it flew past, missing an overhead shot, but connected on the follow-up shot. The bird hit the ground hard and bounced. That pheasant wasn't getting away from us.

Over the winter, I heard occasional rumors from acquaintances who also hunted on the ranch. "They lost the place," was the word. At the beginning of the 1990 season I stopped in and Mrs. Jefferson confirmed the bad news. They managed to reserve a life estate in their residence, but that was it. The new owner wasn't going to let anybody but his friends on the ranch to hunt. She shook her head sadly, adding, "Even I'm going to have to try to find a place to hunt deer."

I drive by the ranch, occasionally, with fond memories of two memorable seasons on this little piece of game paradise. There are signs along the boundary fenceline designating the area as a shooting preserve where people pay money to shoot at pen-raised birds. Changing times.

Returning to the present, Candy and I resumed our hunt. We explored sagebrush patches on the hillside where Jim said he occasionally sees Hungarian partridge, and then followed an irrigation ditch that traces an arc across the contours of the hillside, pushing out another whitetail buck from a clump of sagebrush.

We're back to a little bench overlooking the creek bottom and half a dozen pheasants flush from some heavy sagebrush cover. I pick out a rooster and get a shot off. The pheasant is rocked by the blast of shot and begins to fall, then, making a mid-air somersault, recovers its equilibrium and flies off. I asked an old Army pilot what kind of maneuver that would have been in an airplane. "We'd call that an 'outside loop,'" he said. "It's hard to do and it's hard on the airplane."

We go a little farther in the sagebrush and a cock pheasant flushes at long range, but I manage to scratch it down on my second barrel and I'm gratified to see Candy quickly run the bird down and bring it back to me.

We move back down into the creek bottom and a couple more pheasants flush, and I miss a shot at one quickly-disappearing bird. Then another bird flushes from ahead of me, coming back to give me a couple fast overhead crossing shots at treetop level. I see it crash into the tree branches far overhead. It took a long time to find this bird, but eventually Candy picked it up in grassy cover on the other side of the creek, about 20 feet farther from where I thought it should have hit the ground.

With two birds in the back of my vest and the time approaching 3:30, I figured we've got enough birds for the day and Candy and I begin trudging across a grassy slough on the way back to the truck. Candy, who doesn't know the meaning of quit, puts up another pheasant. I quickly note that it's flying somewhat on the slow side, so I suspect it's the acrobatic bird that I rocked an hour before. In any event, I get an easy crossing shot and there's an explosion of feathers. I can't help but wonder if there's anything left of the bird, but in any event we have our limit of three pheasants.

Before heading home, I stopped to thank Jim for the opportunity to hunt on his land, and I accept his hospitality to come in the house for a cup of coffee.

To tell the truth, I'm not much of a coffee drinker, but one of my principles of hunting is that when a landowner invites me into the house for coffee, I always accept. Sometimes the price of hunting private land is some good conversation.

Back home, it was dark as I finished cleaning pheasants in the back yard (that last bird, incidentally, was well peppered from #6 shot, but still salvageable). It would have been easier if I had gotten home sooner, but there are priorities.

Chapter 18

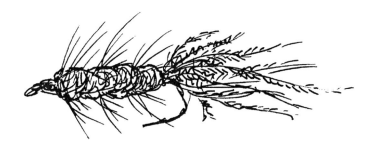

Why Hunt?
My Top Ten List

Why hunt? That's a question that many of us, for whom hunting is as ingrained as part of our being as family, religious faith and favorite football team, must answer.

Hunting is often under attack. We have been and are under attack from animal rights groups and others who consider sport hunting as barbaric. If you don't hunt but do fish, watch out, they're after anglers next. Much criticism is based on the fact that, as our country becomes overwhelmingly urbanized, there are more and more people who see deer, for example, in zoos, or munching on suburban flower gardens, and can't understand how we can hunt these pretty brown-eyed creatures.

Even in the outdoor press, there are those who look at hunting as a dying sport. We only have to look at how *Sports Afield*, one of the great old time hunting and fishing magazines, changed during its last couple years under the Hearst Corporation's ownership. They changed the magazine's emphasis from hunting and fishing to rock climbing, kayaking and other more 'civilized' sports as a cold-blooded business decision. They viewed hunting and fishing as obsolescent activities and moved the magazine's focus to something else.

Every autumn, hunting seasons open across the United States. It's a time of year I eagerly anticipate. The shorter days and crisp nights as summer phases into autumn put an extra bounce in my stride. I look for the first patches of aspen to turn golden on the mountainsides. It's time to get the shotguns out and check the hunting gear for needed repairs. I start dropping birthday hints (mine comes, appropriately, in October) for new products that tend to come in blaze orange or camouflage.

With acknowledgement to David Letterman, I offer my top ten list of reasons we should not only continue hunting, but make sure that our children and grandchildren also learn to hunt, and learn why hunting is an important part of life in the United States.

10. We've got to get them before they get us. Seriously, there is no shortage of game animals. Deer and geese are examples. Some states keep statistics on road-killed deer as a measure of deer populations. This was brought home to me a few years ago when I had a collision with a deer on an Interstate highway. Actually, if you drive across Montana in the fall, you'd wonder, looking at the roadsides, if there could be a living deer or skunk left in the whole state. Excess deer are a serious problem in many areas across the country. Canada geese are the curse of many urban golf courses and parks. At the beginning of the Twentieth Century, wildlife was in danger. In these early years of the 21st Century and after many decades of effective game management, wildlife, with some exceptions, is flourishing—often to a fault.

9. We've got to get them before they get each other. An example is the wildlife crisis of snow geese breeding themselves out of house and home in their arctic nesting grounds along Hudson's Bay. Biologists are desperate to reduce goose numbers, and there really is no alternative other than to hope hunters shoot a lot of geese.

8. The Disney Version. The Disney people are good at what they do, I must admit, as they reduce every good story to a musical cartoon. An example is the venerable *Bambi*, a charming, but virulent piece of anti-hunting propaganda. The Disney Version would have us believe that the animal kingdom is all fun and joy until the evil hunter comes along. I almost choked a few years ago when my younger granddaughter, Madison, climbed into my lap and asked me to read a Disney book about Bambi's rabbit friend, Thumper, who had some sort of problem and went to his friend, Owl, for advice. What crap! What do they think owls eat? Radicchio?

7. Maintain relations between city-dwellers and agriculture. We read the newspaper and watch TV news reports about a crisis in agriculture, and the loss of family farms. It's easy to ignore until we sit in a farmhouse over a cup of coffee and visit with our farmer and rancher friends and see and hear, firsthand, the realities of this crisis.

6. Food has to come from somewhere. Food, whether meat or vegetables, doesn't come from a factory, canned or shrink-wrapped. We once hosted an exchange student from Japan, a real city girl. As far as she was concerned, food did come pre-cut and shrink-wrapped, and was totally grossed out when I cleaned some birds after a successful hunt. Heck, she freaked out when I pulled a carrot out of the garden, brushed off the dirt, and ate it. I suspect her attitudes aren't that much different from that of many American children who grow up never seeing a parent dressing out a duck or pheasant, or hanging a deer in the garage. We can't, realistically, educate all children, but we can make sure our own children understand the realities of life.

5. Death is also a reality and a bullet, once fired, cannot be turned back. Youths should take hunter safety classes and learn about firearms and how to handle them safely. It's important to take them hunting and let them learn, firsthand, that a bullet or a shotgun blast causes death, and that the animal doesn't come back to life after the next commercial.

4. Hunting strengthens family bonds. Raising children isn't always easy and our children's puberty years were difficult. Yet, I can think of no better times than the hunting trips my son and I shared. We didn't always bring home game, but we never had a bad hunt.

3. Hunting is important to America. Only in North America is wildlife considered a public resource. In Europe, game belongs to the landowner, and to the landowner it's a marketable crop. Unfortunately, this is changing in the United States, as trespass fees, pen-raised game birds and animals, hunting preserves, and canned 'hunts' become more prevalent. Only if common citizens keep hunting will we be able to maintain our traditions of wildlife as a public resource.

2. Hunting is a bond we share with wildlife. Without the support of hunters and hunter-supported organizations such as Ducks Unlimited, Rocky Mountain Elk Foundation, or Pheasants Forever or hunter's purchase of Duck Stamps there would be far less wildlife and wildlife habitat. What do anti-hunters do for wildlife?

1. It's more than logic. Hunting is just so darned important. It's pointers and setters, Labrador retrievers, shotguns, prairie winds, mountain sunrises, and more. It's the look of wonderment on a child's face as they discover nature and ask, "Dad, did you see that?" It's seeing a bull elk or wild sheep on a mountain. It's the raucous flush of a pheasant from a brush patch or mallards circling the decoys. Without hunting, we are diminished.

Chapter 19

The Slump

I'm in a slump. Like a baseball player who can't buy a hit, I'm in a slump.

I can pinpoint when the slump began. It was in mid-October, at the end of what had been a great hunting weekend up on Montana's Hi-Line. We wanted one last camping weekend before the expected onset of winter. We camped in the field of a farmer friend and the daily hunts started by simply stepping out the trailer, loading the shotgun and walking.

I had shots at three pheasants on our first morning and I connected on all three of them and had my day's limit before 9 a.m. I was hot that day. All three birds were fast flying cock pheasants that weren't interested in my recreation. But, down they went. I hunted another farm the next day and had my limit of three birds in just 45 minutes from the time I arrived.

On the third day of the weekend, my birthday, incidentally, things were a little tougher, but I had two pheasants by mid-afternoon, and was one bird short of the weekend's possession limit. I took another walk just before sunset and Candy flushed a rooster pheasant from tall grasses. Inexplicably, I fumbled with the gun's safety. I don't know why, because after a couple months of shooting, my gun handling is usually pretty much automatic. By the time I was ready, the pheasant was moving out and I sent a couple ineffective volleys after it. The slump had started.

Hunting is such a psychological sport. If things are going well, I'm bursting with confidence and self-esteem and can do no wrong. But, when in a slump, nothing seems to work.

A week and a half later Candy and I hunted a tract of public land that borders the Beaverhead River. It's about a section in size with a small pond and a spring creek that runs through the end next to the highway, with a meandering slough in the middle. It's a good piece of habitat, though, unfortunately, it gets trashed in those autumns when cattle graze in there.

I spotted a few ducks in the creek when I drove to the gate, so I loaded with steel shot in hopes of connecting with the ducks. The ducks spooked off before we got close, so we continued the walk.

We walked the length of the public land, working various patches of brush, not seeing anything, although Candy would occasionally act like she picked up a scent. At the far end of the cover, Candy started getting excited, and all of a sudden pushed across a little ditch and there was the sound of a flush and I saw a pheasant disappear in the distance.

I called Candy back and counseled her on problems involved with getting out too far.

We worked our way back to where we had started our walk a couple hours earlier and were approaching the pond next to the highway when I looked to see if there were any ducks on the water. I didn't see any so we started walking to the truck. Candy, however, went up to the water's edge and put up a pair of mallards. I kicked myself. If I had stayed with her I would have had a good shot.

I was almost back to the gate when I heard the raucous sounds of a pheasant rooster coming from a brush patch next to where I had just walked. "Tease me, will you. I'll fix your wagon," I thought. We walked back and Candy picked up the bird's scent and put the pheasant up in good range. I shot and missed! It was an easy shot but the bird kept flying. On our walk back to the truck Candy flushed two pheasant hens.

I left Candy home a couple days while I looked for whitetail deer. The river bottoms were crisp and dry from warm weather so walking the bottomlands didn't work. I settled down next to a cottonwood tree and started reading a murder mystery to help pass the time. Flocks of Canada geese flew over my tree. Three wild turkeys emerged from the brush to scratch around in the field behind me. Ants and spiders crawled over me. The heroic detective solved the murder and arrested the perp. I saw only two deer. They stood still while I studied the tops of their heads. Seeing no antlers, I wished them well.

After those unsuccessful deer hunts, I packed the rifle, shotgun and dog and went out for whatever I might find. I scouted a long area of river bottom in the early hours and saw no deer. I hoped to find some waterfowl but they weren't around, either. So, I drove back to that public land where I hunted a couple weeks earlier.

A pair of mallards flushed from the creek. I had an easy shot at the drake and shot both barrels at him. He kept flying. Later, we moved into a brush patch and Candy flushed a big cock pheasant. He went up and swung right by me in his escape flight. I couldn't ask for a better opportunity to collect a pheasant. I emptied both barrels at him and I couldn't believe my eyes when the bird kept flying. I pulled the trigger again, in vain hope that my double-barreled shotgun had somehow morphed into my pumpgun back home, which would have given me a third shot. No such luck.

The next weekend, I left the guns at home and went flyfishing on the Big Hole River, taking advantage of unseasonably mild November weather. The river was crystal clear, sparkling in the late autumn sunshine. I suspect that other people, other places, were also fishing, but Candy and I were totally alone on our stretch of river. I last fished that stretch of river back in late September and had one of my season's better days. This time? *Nada.* Zip. Nothing.

Like the baseball player having a batting slump, the only remedy is to go out and keep swinging until the magic returns. In the meantime, it appeared the fish, birds and deer of Montana were safe from me.

Still, I keep trying. I got permission to hunt on a creek bottom ranch. I have Candy with me and, as it's still early in the afternoon, we take a walk through the heavy cover. We didn't see any pheasants but we chase out a forkhorn whitetail buck and a doe out of a little patch of brushy cover. I decide that things could just possibly get interesting.

With an hour of daylight left I took Candy back to the truck and traded the shotgun for a rifle. I climbed up to the top of a haystack that overlooks the hay meadows in the creek bottom. I spotted a doe looking straight at me and we had a little stare-down until the deer decided I was probably harmless, and she continued feeding as the day faded into the twilight.

I returned the next day, this time leaving Candy at home. I walked through the brush patch where I spotted the forkhorn the day before. I don't see it today, but do spot a small doe. I knelt down next to the fenceline to see what might happen. The deer continued tiptoeing in my direction, approaching to within just 15 yards where it stopped to look at me. She really wanted to see what I was and what I was doing but as long as I was still she couldn't tell what I was. Finally she wandered off.

Back at the truck for a noon sandwich, I belatedly decided to check the state regulations for the area I was in, and found that my tag was good for "either sex whitetail." Darn! I could have gotten my deer, already.

As the sun dropped below the mountain in the western sky I was back at my haystack, and spotted a deer feeding in the alfalfa stubble north of the stack. It was looking straight at me, which didn't present me with much of a shot. Finally, getting a good solid rest, I squeezed off a shot. I thought I could hear the bullet hit.

The deer took off, first running straight toward me, and then veered off into a grassy swale where it disappeared. I hurried over, hoping to find a dead or dying deer. Instead I saw nothing. It was also too dark, by then, to pick up any kind of blood trail.

That evening, incidentally, I went to the local Ducks Unlimited annual dinner where I purchased a black Lab print in the auction and won a .22 rifle in a raffle. A few days later a Kiwanis friend told me that his son was at the banquet, and really was disappointed that he didn't win the rifle. He asked him, "So, who did get it?"

"Aw, some old man."

I'm back the next morning at first light, and I started walking down to the haystack. As I'm walking I saw a deer moving along a fenceline. I took a closer look with my binoculars and it's a buck—a big buck. It is obviously in runt, trotting along with its nose to the ground, intent on doe scent. I watched it jump over the fence to go into a patch of cattails by the creek. Then a moment later it's out of there, going back along the fence.

I'm sorely tempted to lay down in a prone position to take a shot at him, but I'm haunted by the deer I shot at last night. The only ethical thing I can do is to let the buck go off on his sex-driven path and resume my search for last night's doe.

At the edge of the grassy swale where I saw the doe disappear I find a tuft of blood-clotted hair. That means I hit the deer. I search for further signs but come up empty, even after crawling under fences and searching in the brush patch next to the grassy swale.

I kept hunting until dark but saw no more deer. On the drive home I'm really kicking myself. With 20/20 hindsight, I should have passed up that deer of the night before, and I definitely should have tried for that big buck this morning.

A few days later, it's the day before Thanksgiving. I've been frustrated for the last couple weeks because I haven't had any significant upland hunting. I feel like I'm having cabin fever, even though I've spent lots of time hunting deer. The night before, I thought to myself, "I should just get up early and go up to the Rocky Mountain Front and do some pheasant hunting and get things back in order." I mention this to Kay and like the wonderful wife she is, says, "Well, why don't you?"

I was up early the next morning and on the road by 6 a.m. I went to one of the farms I'd hunted the month before, and David met me at the front door, telling me that he had some other people coming within the hour, but suggested a couple isolated CRP fields the family owns, and invited me back for the afternoon.

Candy and I checked out the CRP and walked the cover and the net result of the morning was one hen pheasant that Candy flushed from light cover.

We returned to the farm in early afternoon and David says that the other hunters were gone and I was welcome to hunt.

I parked at the edge of the farmstead and we begin walking the perimeter of the 160 acre stubble field. In a brushy corner, half a dozen hens flush, which got Candy excited.

We walked along the north side of the field and halfway down the fenceline, Candy locked on a scent in thin cover. She finally lunged and a big cock pheasant took to the air, giving me a right to left quartering-away shot. I shot and the pheasant went down. Candy had trouble getting through the sheep-tight fence, but I helped her through and she retrieved the bird.

I felt like a weight has been lifted from my shoulders, as this time

I finally capitalized on the opportunity and brought the bird down. This turned out to be a quite a long-tailed bird, as well. I noted the time. It's 1:13 p.m.

We turn the corner to the east side of the field and Candy again locked up on a scent, this time putting up a hen (though I'm not entirely convinced that it's not a rooster).

We reach a brushy corner, a favorite spot, and surprisingly, we don't find any birds in there. However we work the cover along a little creek that runs along the fenceline. We flush several birds in there, including a rooster that I miss.

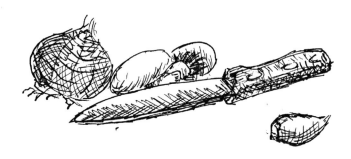

We get to another corner at the edge of sheep pens near the farm buildings where all hell breaks loose with birds flushing from the edge of the weedy cover. One is a rooster that I miss, and then another. A small rooster flushes and I hit it with my first shot, and then hit it again, but the bird keeps flying, going across the road, struggling to stay aloft. It keeps struggling to fly, and then just before it went out of sight at the top of the rise, it looks like it dived to the ground. Candy saw the bird go down and headed out there, but didn't go far enough before coming back. She actually tried several times but didn't understand retrieving from a long distance, as well the inconvenient fact that the bird fell on the neighboring farm where I don't have permission to hunt.

We re-traced our path along the fenceline creek and, sure enough, there are still a few birds in there that we missed the first time. One is a rooster that I managed to knock down before it got away. It lands very much alive and Candy went for it. I could see it jump and then Candy looked back to give me a puzzled look, as if to say, "Where'd it go?"

I see it again about 15 feet from where it had jumped and I shoot it again to plant it. This time Candy is able to pick it up and brings it back. One more bird to go for our limit.

We go back through the trees and the cattail slough in the corner of the field. Candy disappears in a little clump of cattails where irrigation water drains off into a corner. I could hear her crashing around in the cattails and then I heard a plunge when she jumped into a hole full of water. Suddenly a pheasant pops out and he's flying hard to make his escape. I bring him down with my first shot and Candy makes the retrieve. It's 1:53 p.m. and we have our limit of pheasants.

It's about a half hour walk back to the truck. The three pheasants in my vest are heavy, but it's a good heavy.

The next day is Thanksgiving and I feel I have much for which to be thankful. Kay had to work, so I stayed home to roast one of the previous day's pheasants, complemented with a *sauce smitane* (from *Joy of Cooking*), and bake an apple pie. It was a festive dinner for the two of us.

The slump was over.

Chapter 20

Ol' Blue's Last Hunt

An important partner in any outing, whether it's for fishing, hunting or just to see autumn colors, is the car or truck we use for transportation. It's a big event when we get a new vehicle.

We don't trade vehicles very often; hate to make payments, I guess. Nevertheless, we just closed a deal to replace the truck we've been driving since 1990. It's a blue half-ton pickup and it has served us well but we decided it was time to move up a few years.

I don't know where the time went since we went to the local dealer to take delivery of the truck. "It's really pretty," said the salesman. We had ordered it from the factory just the way we wanted it, several months before, and we impatiently waited through the summer for it to work its way through the manufacturing and transportation pipeline.

Our previous hunting/fishing/camping vehicle was a 1977 International Scout and I still have sentimental thoughts about the old Scout. It was a prototype for the sport utility vehicles that have become so popular in recent years. Those old Scouts were noisy and boxy, but they held a lot of cargo and could pull a good size trailer, to boot. We put that cargo capacity to the test, time and again, when our children grew up and went to college.

Incidentally, a predecessor to the Scout was a 1969 Volkswagen Squareback. The Squareback was ahead of its time, with a computerized fuel injection system that, unfortunately, had a tendency to not start at inconvenient times. Even when it did run the interior was cold in winter and hot in summer, though I had to give it credit for going through just about anything if you could just get it going. It was a happy day when we traded it off. Years later I perused a book of famous automotive lemons. The VW Squareback was included.

Getting back to my story, those Scouts did have a design problem that eventually showed up on just about every one on the road. Their fenders were vulnerable to corrosion and eventually they all looked like rust buckets, even if you didn't live in Minnesota or Wisconsin where they spread layers of salt on the roads after every snowfall.

We had many good times with the Scout, though a vivid memory was not one of Scout's better moments. In 1987, I drew a North Dakota spring turkey permit. In scouting my hunting area, I found a tract of state-owned woodland. A dirt road went across the area, fording a little stream at the bottom of a valley.

Spring runoff made that dirt road impassable for a couple weeks, but it finally dried out enough to drive down the road. I got to the ford and started driving across. The front wheels were beginning to climb out when the engine stalled. The exhaust pipe had gone under water and I learned that engines stop running when that happens. I opened the door to assess the situation and a surge of water flooded the interior.

I got to shore and hiked to a nearby farm. The farmer got a funny grin on his face as he went out to start his tractor. "I pull a turkey hunter out of there every spring," he said. I was just the lucky guy who made his season complete.

The blue truck was quite a step up in the world from old Scout. Factory air, stereo, comfortable seats, a good ride—a far cry from the old Studebaker truck I learned to drive back on the farm, years ago.

It had taken us all over Montana and adjacent states, plus longer trips east to Chicago and west to the Coast. It hauled camping trailers to favorite campsites, again and again. I don't know how many times it took us to the Big Hole River for fishing, all over Montana for hunting, and frequent ski trips. Though I'm not much of an elk hunter, I brought five elk home in the back of the truck, plus several deer, and, I'd guess, hundreds of pheasants, ducks and other assorted birds.

The truck had its closest call a couple seasons ago, while en route to a duck hunt. The highway was slick ice from freezing rain and I was creeping along in four-wheel drive. A car coming from the opposite direction lost control as it approached and began fishtailing in a direct collision course. I decided the better option was to take the ditch, but braced for a collision. Somehow, we avoided the crash by inches and, luckily, had no problem getting out of the ditch.

Ol' Blue's last hunt turned out to be one of those long hikes in the aspens. Candy put up just one grouse and I didn't get a shot at it, so the walk back to the truck was a weary trudge.

Still, when I emerged from the trees and saw the truck gleaming in the autumn sunshine, I couldn't help but recall the salesman's words, over 13 years earlier, "It's really pretty."

Chapter 21

The Dog Who Went to War

We'd had a great morning. Candy and I made two successful sneaks on ducks on a spring creek and with three shots I got three drake mallards. Now, we were struggling through a particularly nasty river bottom jungle, in what looked like a fruitless struggle. Suddenly, I heard wings and the raucous scolding of a pheasant rooster as it flew off.

"It's too far off," was my first thought. Then instinct overruled logic as my shotgun went to my shoulder and I pulled the trigger. To my surprise, the bird folded. Now I thought, "How will we ever find that bird?"

Candy didn't see the bird fall, but I gestured off in the general direction and said, "Candy! Go get the bird." She trotted off and a minute later came back with the pheasant. "Good girl!" I said, and praised her for her retrieving talent. "All in a day's work," her body language said, as she went off in search of more birds.

On the drive home, I recalled other dogs in my life, and these memories always begin with Shep.

I have no personal memories of Pearl Harbor, as I was just two years old at the time. A memory from some mid-point of the war, however, is of two Army men dressed in summer tans coming to the farm to get our dog. We had a male German shepherd and my father had volunteered him for military service.

On a cloudy day in March, several years later, I went with Dad to the local train station. After doing his turn in the Army K9 Corps, Shep was coming home. There were questions about bringing the dog home. Would he still remember his farm family? After intensive training as a military guard dog, could he still be a family dog?

The first question was answered when we opened the shipping crate and the big dog jumped up to lick Dad on the face. From the back seat of the family car, he kept licking Dad's face all the way home. There was certainly no question about his being happy to be back. Dad really knew Shep was home after milking cows that evening. When Dad finished running the fresh, creamy milk through strainers into milk cans, Shep waited patiently for Dad to break down the equipment for cleaning. Shep begged for a strainer pad just like he always had.

As to the second question, there seemed to be more questions than answers. The Army, in correspondence that preceded Shep's return, told us that guard dogs were 'de-trained' before they could be returned to their civilian families.

We soon learned that, in spite of de-training, some aspects of guard training were too ingrained to be forgotten. This was brought home to us one afternoon after school. While Dad was milking and doing chores, my brother, Carl, and I were playing "cops and robbers" in the barn. Carl pointed a wooden gun at me.

Suddenly, he found himself on his back. Shep's training took over when Carl pointed the gun and he leaped up, pushed Carl down and took the toy gun away from him. Shep was actually quite gentle the way he did it, but he certainly made it clear that nobody pointed guns, and he would enforce the rules.

I'd like to tell how Shep lived a long and happy civilian life, but it wasn't to be. My mother taught piano, so there was a regular stream of neighborhood kids that came for lessons after school. Richard, for some reason, was scared of Shep. One day, after his lesson, he went outside while his sister had her lesson and came by the barn to see what we were up to.

As Richard approached us, he saw Shep, turned around and ran. This triggered Shep's training that anyone running away is a bad guy. He ran him down, giving him a nip in the shoulder in the process.

Richard wasn't really hurt, but our parents decided that the risk of having a guard dog around neighborhood children was too great, so they regretfully took him to the veterinarian to be euthanized.

In the following years, we had several more dogs on the farm, and for over 40 years, Labrador retrievers have been part of our family and valued hunting partners. Nevertheless, Shep will always have a special place in my memory as our family dog that went to war.

Chapter 22

Victory Pheasants

A Look Back at a Not-So-Distant Past

The war was suddenly over, and a nation paused and began to relax.

No one appreciated the pause more than Bill Antonioli. A native of Butte, Montana, he was a medical student at the University of Michigan and the pressure had been relentless. Except for short vacations at Christmas, he hadn't had a break in several years. "There's a war on, you know." Medical school was a meat grinder of uninterrupted studies, in anticipation that each year's graduating physicians would be urgently needed near the front lines to repair the never-ending waves of battle casualties.

In August 1945, the war was suddenly over, and the medical school scheduled a six-day break at the end of October. Bill decided to go pheasant hunting. With his intense academic schedule, he hadn't had many hunting opportunities, except a few weekends in Michigan. With six days off, he could get a real outing.

He'd read magazine articles telling of pheasant hunting in South Dakota, so he studied train schedules, picked a destination on a branch line of the old Milwaukee Road, and at a cost of $20, booked round-trip train tickets for a journey from Ann Arbor, Michigan to South Dakota.

From the vantage point of 2011, 1945 was a different time. The nation, recovering from the Depression, had plunged into a world war. By war's end, the armies of the world were using jet planes, dropping nuclear bombs, and sending guided missiles toward enemy cities. Yet, in rural America, not much had changed. Most roads were still unpaved. Plane travel was a rare adventure. In those pre-Amtrak days, however, you could get on a train and literally go anywhere.

This was also a legendary pheasant-hunting period. Pheasant numbers began expanding around the Midwest in the 1920s, and, in the 1940s, bird populations exploded. Most hunters were fighting other battles around the globe, and few people back home had time to hunt, and would have had difficulty getting shotgun shells, or justifying using precious gasoline and tire ration stamps on recreation. For those with an opportunity to hunt, however, this was a bonanza era.

The sun was falling as Bill got off the train in Tripp, a small town in southeastern South Dakota. With a suitcase in one hand and a Winchester Model 12 20-gauge pumpgun in the other, he spotted a hotel in the middle of town. He checked in at the hotel and booked several nights lodging, at $3 per night, in one of the hotel's 10 rooms (the bathroom was down the hall).

The owner of the hotel noted Bill's shotgun and asked, "Were you planning to hunt? You're going to need a license, so you'd better talk to Henry."

He directed Bill to go across the street and find Henry Voss, the local game warden, to buy his hunting license.

Bill found Henry, and bought a non-resident hunting license for $20. Henry looked at him and asked, "So, what's your plan?"

"I guess I'll walk out past the edge of town and start hunting," Bill said.

"Well, you might be able to get a few birds that way," Henry said, "but, if you can wait until around 9:00, I'll come and pick you up and we'll see what we can do."

True to his word, Henry picked him up at 9 a.m., and the two of them went pheasant hunting, together. At that time, hunters, especially during the war years, were relatively few. It was almost unknown for landowners to hang a 'No Trespassing' sign on their fences. A common and proven method to hunt pheasants was to 'road hunt.'

Recalling his long ago pheasant hunt, Bill says, "There was some sort of 'one foot on the ground' rule that applied to road hunters." Continuing, he relates, "Henry would drive down the back roads, and if he'd spot the head of a pheasant sticking above the grain stubble or roadside cover, he'd slam on the brakes, open the car door and by the time he had one foot on the ground, he'd be shooting."

The next two days, three more hunters joined Bill and Henry. Captain Orlo Jackson, a young Army officer in the process of returning to civilian life, and his father and younger brother, all strangers to the area, had found their way to Tripp, South Dakota, and came under the helpful wing of Warden Henry Voss.

With five hunters working together, they collaborated on classic midwestern pheasant hunting strategies. They hunted harvested cornfields, with several hunters walking down the corn rows, with others waiting at the end of the field. "Every time, when we got to the end of the field, it seemed," Bill recalls, "150-200 pheasants would get up."

They also hunted heavy cover in cattail sloughs scattered around the fields, and again they put up flocks of pheasants from the cover.

As an oddity, in one clump of brush, they flushed a covey of guinea hens that had either escaped from pens or had been released and reverted to the wild.

For three days, the shooting was fast and furious. Bill didn't consider himself a great shot, but with these shooting opportunities, he had no trouble coming up with his possession limit of 24 pheasants, based on limits of 12 birds (either sex) per day. He sent the birds, cleaned and packed in ice, on a westbound train to his mother back in Montana. At Christmas time, two months later, he had another week off from medical school and traveled home to dine on some of his South Dakota pheasants.

Since 1945 much has changed. South Dakota is still a great pheasant state. Much of the land in farm country is, however, virtually closed to strangers. Unless you're hiring a guide or have inside connections in pheasant country, it may be difficult to get permission to chase pheasants in South Dakota. Back in '45, as Bill recalls, farmers mainly just pointed off to a nearby field and said something like, "I just saw a big bunch out there."

I suspect a game warden in any state, nowadays, would lose his or her job if they took it on themselves to just go hunting for a few days with some strangers from out of state. As for taking the train, the Milwaukee Road bellied up back in the '70s, and today's Amtrak doesn't go to South Dakota.

Another contrast to today's pheasant hunts was the lack of dogs. In 1945, relatively few midwestern pheasant hunters had gun dogs. Again, we were emerging from the Depression and the War years. If someone had a dog along for the hunt, it was more than likely a farm dog of varying lineage described, most likely, as a "shepherd." As a postscript, in 1950, the country was again at war, this time in a far-off place called Korea. Bill was back home in Montana with a young family and a new private practice. The U.S. Government sent Bill a letter offering him the option of enlisting in the Army Medical Corps as a commissioned officer, or to be drafted as a private. He accepted a commission, and after requesting assignment to the Far East, was, naturally, sent to Europe.

Years later, on a family vacation, he returned to Tripp, South Dakota to take another look at his old hunting grounds. The hotel was still there. Warden Henry Voss was gone, but Bill found his 90-year old widow and visited her, sharing fond memories of Henry and their hunt of years before. "Henry knew everybody, and knew the country like the back of his hand," Bill recalls, "and, my, how he loved to hunt."

Chapter 23

Mysteries

I don't remember what drew me that first time to that corner of the ridge that separates a pair of merging creek bottoms. Two old log buildings next to the creek, slowly disintegrating back into the mountainside, are all that's left of an old mining camp except for piles of rock, debris and rusting machinery that mark where miners a century ago dredged their way through the valley in search of precious metals. Nature is slowly reclaiming the creek bottoms and willows and aspens grow thick in and near the old rock piles.

Next to a thicket of aspen trees something white caught my eye. Going closer, I could see that it was a gravesite. The cross-shaped tombstone was concrete and the date, November 4, 1908, had been inscribed. A piece of metal with the words, "OUR DARLING," embossed on it, was set into the concrete. A low picket fence outlined the grave, a child's grave most likely by the outline of the fence. Surprisingly, it was still white enough so that it must have been painted sometime in the last few years. Were there still family members in the area who cherished the memory of the woman who died, nearly a century ago, at the onset of winter? Had other hunters, like me, come across the grave and taken it upon themselves to maintain it?

I try to return to the grave every year to pay my respects to the memory of this child who devastated her family with her premature death.

* * * * *

Something white under a clump of willows caught my eye in the North Dakota creek bottom where I was hunting ruffed grouse. A sun-bleached deer skull with a set of trophy-class antlers in good condition marked where a whitetail deer died the previous winter. Had he been wounded by a hunter and successfully managed to escape, only to bleed to death in his hiding place? Perhaps he just reached the end of the line and died quietly on some sub-zero winter night.

A year before, less than a mile up the valley, another trophy white-tail buck made the mistake of walking in front of me at the opening moment of the deer season. These two deer were likely related, possibly brothers, and had without doubt sparred for the favors of does during previous rutting seasons. Just as they once shared habitat, they continue to look at each other from adjoining walls of our family room.

* * * * *

Walking across the prairies of northern Montana in search of pheasants, a rock caught my eye. It was piece of native sandstone, shaped so that it could be strapped with rawhide thongs to a stout handle; a simple but fearsome war club. The Blackfeet ruled these plains in the days before farmers and ranchers brought 'progress' to the area. Did this rock mark where a skirmish had taken place? Did the club's owner mete out punishment to an enemy, or did he meet his own end, with the stone marking where he fell? Whatever happened, the rock was the only sign that something had happened on this spot a long time ago. Black, orange, and bluish-gray lichens on the rock bear witness to many passing seasons.

I recently showed that rock to a neighbor, a retired biology professor who spent many years teaching at Montana State University-Northern, Havre. While he didn't say that some Native American hadn't used that rock as a convenient weapon, his immediate reaction was that it was a vertebra from a dinosaur. It's an open question as to whether this solves the mystery or only deepens it.

* * * * *

I was walking along the banks of a creek in another North Dakota ruffed grouse covert, thick with hawthorns, alders and aspens, and was surprised to see an old pair of wooden skis, almost completely hidden by grass and other vegetation. Many years had passed since the mystery skier stood there. The trees were thick enough that it would have been impossible to ski through the brush to that spot now.

More than likely, the skier was not there for recreation. These skis were likely working transportation for a trapper or hunter, or even a worker from the nearby farm. But, why did he leave his skis? Did he get turned around while attending to his rounds and forget where he took them off? Was he caught in a thaw so that it was easier to walk home than struggle with sticky spring snow? Why didn't he come back for his skis?

* * * * *

"We can shoot pheasants anywhere," said the Iowa farmer's son. "But if we shoot a quail from Mama's house covey, she'll kill us." I had just gotten acquainted with his father a couple days earlier in a chance business conversation. When I asked if I could hunt pheasants on their eastern Iowa farm, he said, "Sure." This became a favorite hunting spot, not just because of the pheasant hunting, but because hunting here made you part of the family, and the farmer or one of his sons frequently took time to join me on the hunt.

On the field sloping away from the farmhouse was a knoll with a little clump of trees. In this intensively farmed area, it was unusual to see trees in the middle of a field. The farmer's son and I went over to investigate. In the trees was a cracked and weathered headstone marking the burial place of a woman, with the dates, 1797 – 1835.

In Montana, where I now live, the time of the frontier to the present can sometimes be measured in a span of as little as three generations. In the middle of this Iowa cornfield rested the remains of a woman born when George Washington was President and died when a future president, Abraham Lincoln, was still a country lawyer in the neighboring state of Illinois. Did she die in childbirth? Worn by the rigors of pioneer life, did she die of a premature old age? We can only wonder.

No doubt this woman was familiar with guns and a flintlock fowling piece probably accompanied the pioneer family to the Iowa prairies. Roast prairie chicken or bobwhite quail would have been a welcome change from salt pork or dried venison. Possibly, she might have been the one in the family with the occasional opportunity to steal away from the log cabin, gun in hand, to get fresh meat for supper. We said a silent prayer for the memory of this pioneer woman and slipped away to resume the hunt.

It has been many years since we left Iowa, but my mind often returns to that special place where the memory of this pioneer woman was respected and cherished, and Mama's house covey was off limits.

Chapter 24

Preserving Hunting Memories

On Sunday, September 22, 1985, I skipped church and went grouse hunting. I had been in meetings in Denver all week, and my nerves were frazzled. I needed a retreat and Alix, my then 8-month-old chocolate Labrador retriever needed to learn about ruffed grouse.

A week before, she had her introduction to sharp-tailed grouse on the opening day of the North Dakota upland bird season. On our very first walk through the grassland, Alix suddenly veered into the breeze and flushed a covey of grouse. I emptied my Weatherby pumpgun at the departing birds, missing with all three shots. While I hastily reloaded, a straggler flushed, and I managed to wing it.

Alix went over to where the bird fell. The bird jumped up and tried to fly away. Alix jumped back. After several more bird jump-dog jumps, Alix worked up her courage to put a paw on the bird and hold it down while she figured out what to do next. She finally decided to pick up the bird and bring it to me. By noon, we had collaborated for two more sharptails for our limit of three birds.

With that opening day introduction to upland bird hunting, I was anxious to hit the ruffed grouse coverts. It was an overcast day with temperatures in the mid-50s. A few trees were beginning to show fall colors.

We came home with one ruffed grouse, a mature brown-phase bird, plus we flushed two more. I also found a clump of wild raspberries that still had some fruit, and enjoyed a snack before we resumed our wanderings in the creek bottom. Our wanderings went a bit astray at one point, as I got "momentarily confused" about just where we were. A soft rain began falling as we left the aspens.

Now, my point isn't to show that I'm a great hunter or dog trainer, and you have already figured out I'm not a great shot. You probably don't give a rip that I skipped church one Sunday (okay, maybe that wasn't the only Sunday), over 20 years ago, to go grouse hunting.

What I am suggesting is that you make a New Year's Resolution. You must understand, of course, that New Year's Day isn't January 1. New Year's Day is the opening day of the hunting season. The resolution I suggest you make is to start a hunting diary, so you can preserve your memories of the hunt.

I had never kept a diary and the thought of a hunting journal seemed just a tad strange when I first saw reference to one, years ago, in George Bird Evans' classic book, *An Upland Shooting Life*. In an introduction to the 1971 edition of the book, Evans noted that he had been keeping a gun diary since 1932.

Like most New Year's resolutions, it took awhile before I actually made one of my own and actually took action to carry it out. I started keeping a hunting diary in 1985. This seemed an appropriate time to begin. Sam, my black Lab partner since 1970, died the previous October, and starting a hunting diary at the beginning of Alix's career seemed fitting.

In my first entry, I noted that I "surplused" this bound book of blank pages from my office. I didn't think it would be missed. In the previous 12 years that this book had been in my office stockroom, the only use it had ever had was when someone ripped out a few pages for some long-forgotten emergency.

It took three seasons to fill that first book. Since then, I filled another (I actually bought that one at a bookstore), and since 1992 have made my diary entries with a computer. A computer isn't very artistic, as these things go, I suppose, but the printed page generated by a modern word processing program is a lot more legible than my handwriting. I've never had good penmanship, but what I have now is mostly indecipherable. I know, because often I have to figure out my notes from an interview of just the day before. I wrinkle my brow, stare at my notes, and say, "Huh?"

In these past seasons, the books and loose-leaf binders I have filled with my notes on various hunts have become priceless. I often refer back to my notes on some long-ago hunt and suddenly find myself lost in memories of outings that would, otherwise, just be part of a fuzzy past.

From those first two hunts I made with Alix, when she was a three-quarter grown pup, I can progress to her first duck and pheasant hunts to September 10, 1997, when she collapsed after a short walk in a Montana grouse covert, marking the beginning of the end of her career. Some memories are sweet. Some are bittersweet.

My diaries also chronicle outings with several hunting partners. In the fall of 1987, I hunted several times with John, a lawyer whose office was next door to mine. We had known each other for a long time, but had never hunted together until that autumn. Not long after those hunts, I accepted a transfer to Montana, and several years later, John died from an unexpected heart attack. It has been a long time since those hunts back in 1987, but a look through those old diary scribblings brings it all back.

How do you start a hunting diary? Well, as they say, "Just do it." Get a book, or use a computer, or whatever writing tool is comfortable for you. You can buy bound books of blank pages at many bookstores. Some catalog companies, such as Orvis, sell hunting diaries that make the job easier with printed checklists for entering information.

The hardest part of maintaining a hunting diary is disciplining oneself to make the entries. I often find myself playing catch-up, trying to sort out the details of several hunts at the same time, and hoping I've gotten it all straight. Some of my longer written accounts are, not surprisingly, those I've written the same day or the next day, when the highlights of the day's hunt are still fresh in my mind. When I've neglected my diary I find myself playing catch-up, and pinning down the precise day of an outing is as difficult as sorting out my memories of the day.

My diary entries record more than words. I've taped in tailfeathers, or made an occasional sketch of some humorous sight. I have no artistic talent, but it doesn't take a lot of talent to sketch the sight of an aspen sapling that I just decapitated, while the grouse that I was hoping to bag disappeared into the forest.

Keeping a hunting diary probably won't make you a better hunter. It certainly won't improve your shooting, and your dog won't care one way or the other. Your diaries will likely have no intrinsic value.

On the other hand, as the years accumulate, your diary will increase in value to yourself, and can form a priceless record to pass on to your children or grandchildren. I recently heard, for example, of an elderly man who, upon his death, left his son a wonderful legacy—a diary of his 60 years of flyfishing the streams of western Montana.

I've spent many days hunting and fishing in recent years with a friend 10 years older than I. Like my late lawyer friend from North Dakota, his name is also John. During our many drives across the countryside, he's told many great stories.

Unfortunately, like most, he has never made any record of his outings and one of these days his memories will fade and disappear.

Start a hunting diary this fall. You may feel uncomfortable, at first, with this new "affectation." One season's hunting may not mean much, but as the seasons come and go, you'll find your diary will increase in value. Your journal will let you relive long-ago hunts, smile with the memories of a dog's first hunt, and, perhaps, you'll shed a tear or two as you recall dogs or hunting partners who now live only in the pages of your hunting diary.

Chapter 25

Coverts

A covert, whether or not you pronounce the "t" (either is correct, according to my dictionary) is a term most often associated with ruffed grouse hunting. I suppose it's because in grouse hunting, more than other types of hunting, we direct our hunts to specific areas that have suitable grouse habitat. I occasionally give these coverts names. These names probably have no significance to anyone but me, but do help me keep things straight.

Often other people who write about ruffed grouse use "cover" instead of "covert." I personally prefer covert, though I'll pronounce it with that silent "*t.*"

It sometimes takes awhile to give a new covert a name, but eventually, it'll find its identity. I found a new covert last fall. I guess it's not new to others, but it was new to me, at least. I had often wondered where a dirt road went after it left the highway. I had driven by the turnoff many times but never followed up my curiosity with action.

On a frosty, sunny, September morning, I finally took the turnoff, hoping the road would reveal a new covert.

My expectations that the area was not new to others were quickly confirmed when I drove by somebody's hunting camp, a camping trailer parked along a creek. I followed the road to the top of a mountain ridge where two vehicles were parked. Presumably, the absentee owners of those vehicles were archery hunters from the creek-side camp and were out searching for elk. I drove back down to the valley and parked on a wide spot off the road overlooking a brushy creek bottom that led to a valley spotted with groves of quaking aspen.

As a younger hunter, I didn't know beans about ruffed grouse, but after years of pursuing them I've developed a sense for ruffed grouse habitat. My suspicions are often rewarded with the sight or sound of ruffed grouse taking wing. On good days, I'm additionally rewarded with shots at birds and occasional birds in the back of my vest.

The creek was just a tiny seep of water, but there were occasional beaver dams that created a series of pools. The ground was carpeted with moose droppings, something I consider a good indicator for ruffed grouse habitat.

The creek bottom branched off into several drainages as we gained altitude. I followed the branch that hugged the side of the mountain and narrowed as Candy and I climbed up the canyon.

In the middle of a clump of pines, I entered a tiny clearing where there sat the moldering remains of an old log cabin, with a rusty bedspring marking where a one-time prospector or woodcutter spent some cozy, or miserable, winter nights.

Just as we reached the top of the drainage, Candy and I were rewarded with a rush of wings and the glimpse of a ruffed grouse disappearing into the trees. A moment later another grouse flushed. I got off a couple hurried shots before it disappeared up the hillside. Candy searched for a downed bird, but came up empty.

From the top of this drainage, it was a short walk across the hillside to reach the next aspen-covered draw. There turned out to be a lot of cover in this draw, but we didn't flush any birds until we worked our way down to the bottom. There, in a jungle of beaver-downed aspens, vines, thistles and other undergrowth, a grouse flushed just a few feet from me, vanishing before I had a chance to react.

All in all, this little valley was big enough for a three-hour walk and I established that it holds ruffed grouse. There are a couple more draws probably worth checking out on future trips, but the frosty morning had changed to a hot and dry afternoon and it was time to go home.

This covert doesn't have a name yet, but we'll let that problem take care of itself. The bottom line is that I found a new grouse covert and that's always a good morning's work, one that should pay off in coming years.

A creek bottom back in North Dakota, where I first encountered ruffed grouse, was next to a gravel pit, so naturally that became the Gravel Pit covert. It took a few trips before things connected, but I eventually figured out that when someone was working the gravel pit, with the roar of front end loaders and the beep-beep-beep of machinery backing up, the grouse were usually scarce. We'd see more grouse when the machinery was silent.

I once followed a dirt track across a flax field and found an all but hidden valley behind it. That covert became, naturally, the Flax Field covert, though that was the only year the farmer ever grew flax in that field.

Another dirt road went up a hillside, past a stack of beehives, and ended in a clearing on the edge of an aspen and oak forest along the escarpment marking the western edge of the Red River Valley. I recall a couple incidents that made the Bee Hive memorable.

Kevin, then a teenager, and I were hunting the Bee Hive on a Saturday morning. We'd made a wide circle through the trees and brush, not moving any birds. I declared a rest break, and Kevin and I sat on a log while we ate a candy bar and had an extended discussion on some relevant topic. Sam, our black Lab, enjoyed the rest, but soon decided it was time to resume the hunt. We picked up our guns and took a few steps, flushing a grouse that had been there all along, just a few feet from where we'd been talking and laughing for the prior 15 minutes.

On another day, a warm and sunny October afternoon, I came back to the parking place in the clearing and found my International Scout covered with dozens of strange-looking insects I later learned were called 'walking sticks.' I'd never seen them before or since but there were all sorts of them that day.

Another hidden valley became known as Moose Valley, when I came around a bend in the creek bottom and found myself face to face with a cow moose.

A couple other coverts happened to be contained in a state-owned wildlife management area, so a name of my own choosing might seem overkill. Still, one of them acquired a name, anyway. Following an old trail up a hillside, we'd come to the site of a long-abandoned farmstead, since grown up to long grass and brush. An old basement of a house was marked by a depression in the ground containing rotted boards and glass jars. Lilac bushes still stood next to what was probably a doorway years ago. A little way from the house was an old well that had been reinforced with wood cribbing. The cribbing had long decomposed, but the well shaft was still square, marking the work of long-ago pioneers.

Across the meadow from the old house was an aged log barn still standing at the edge of a chokecherry thicket. A small tree had been cut and nailed to the side of the barn, creating a rustic ladder to a small haymow on the upper level of the barn. This hunting area, naturally, became known as the Log Barn covert.

The Log Barn was a productive covert and provided many thrills, particularly one year—a banner year for grouse. Sam, working an aspen jungle along the trail to the barn, flushed at least half a dozen grouse, one at a time, across our path. I'd rather not try to remember if we downed any of those birds, but we had our thrills.

I also remember the Log Barn for another incident. Mike, one of my co-workers, was chatting about the prior weekend when his brother, Jerry, stopped at his house for a visit. Mike's wife, Angela, served a graham cracker crust pie for dessert. The brother loved the pie and said, "I love graham cracker crust pies. I could eat moose shit if it came in a graham cracker crust."

Mike and I had a good laugh over this, but the last laugh was yet to come. The following weekend I was hunting the Log Barn and noticed where a moose had paused in its travels. It wasn't far from the Scout, so I retrieved a sandwich bag and collected a baggie-full, more than sufficient for a pie.

I delivered the baggie to Mike, and he and Angela bought a piecrust and the next weekend they invited Jerry to come over for dessert. He regarded the treat with disdain, growling, "I'm going to get you for this."

Mike replied, "Sorry, but you were the one who suggested it in the first place."

In a dozen years, I'd 'acquired' a collection of coverts. The names, such as the Log Barn and Gardar Homestead and the Old Homestead, had a common theme, as the aspen thickets near these old abandoned farmsteads seemed a magnet for grouse. Of course, the homesteads also bore witness to changing rural economies, lost dreams and memories. I'd look into the broken windows of an abandoned house and wonder just how long it was since people had lived there. I'd often wonder whether the former occupants were still alive and whether their memories of their old home were happy ones.

Aside from autumnal woolgathering, the important thing was

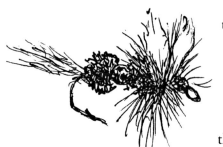

that, in a prairie state better known for waterfowl and pheasants, I found my own little paradise, or a collection of paradises, to be specific, for ruffed grouse.

The problem with many jobs is that sooner or later you have to move and all those years of collecting grouse coverts go down the drain.

The mountain country of southwestern Montana is better known for elk and flyfishing than ruffed grouse. Still, when I was fishing a little creek near the Mule Ranch, I looked across the valley to aspen thickets on the hillside a couple miles away and thought, "I'll bet there are grouse back there."

The Mule Ranch was exactly that back in the heyday of underground mining in Butte. Mules were trussed up and taken down the mineshafts and into the drifts of the Butte Hill to haul cars full of copper ore to where it could be elevated to the surface. Those mining tunnels, far below the ground's surface, were the mules' home for months at a time. Periodically, however, the mules would be rotated out of the mines and trucked out to the Mule Ranch for rest and rehabilitation in the lush grassy pastures of the Pintler Mountains.

September finally came and Alix, the chocolate Lab that followed Sam, and I headed for the aspens, hoping for grouse. This became the first episode in a story I think of as the Jinx of the Mule Ranch.

Alix flushed a grouse almost right away. I had a clear shot and I'd swear I saw the bird go down. Alix and I looked all over for the bird but we couldn't find any sign of it. We moved a couple more grouse, but didn't get any more shooting.

A season later we returned. Alix flushed a grouse from next to an old beaver pond. I shot and missed. We followed the bird into the aspens and I got two more shots, this time succeeded in dropping an aspen branch. I began to sense a jinx.

Do hunting spots carry a jinx? It seems that way at times. I'm not Superman. I miss my share of shots. Still, at the end of the hunting season, I usually have birds in the freezer, so I know that my dogs and I can bring home the bacon. Why then, do some spots seem jinxed?

It's probably coincidence. Over the course of the season we're bound to have a few off days and it's just dumb luck when those bad days keep turning up in the same spots.

Shotgunning is, however, a psychological game. If you feel lucky, it seems that every time a bird gets up it's no trick at all. Flush. Bang! Retrieve. Why do we make such a big deal out of it? On the other hand, if you fall into a slump there's no hope. Flush. Bang! "Damn!" Flush. Bang! Bang! "Damn!"

Maybe it's no accident that a grouse covert or pheasant patch gets jinxed. If you have bad luck in a particular spot, you're likely to go back half-convinced you're going to fail—a self-fulfilling prophecy if there ever was one.

Still, there is hope. In the eighth season of pounding the Mule Ranch covert, with several seasons of not seeing any birds at all, it seemed like the covert was stiff with grouse. After four flushes (hmmm, does that make me a four flusher?) I got off a successful shot (an earlier shot put a two inch notch in the side of an aspen tree) and Alix followed the flight of the bird and came back with a lightly hit grouse. I said to myself, "I've finally broken the jinx of the Mule Ranch covert."

The Mule Ranch may have its jinx, but that hasn't stopped me from finding more grouse spots and several have earned names. The Old Mine covert is a creek bottom that was sluice-mined a century ago and has since grown up into willows, aspen and other brush. Mother Nature is doing her best to heal the scars of mining, though piles of rock all over the area defy Nature's best efforts.

The whisper of water on another hillside drew me to its sound. Springs near the top gushed a steady flow of water that streamed down the hillside. The shallow water was choked with watercress. I often return to the springs, and usually remember to take a plastic bag along.

Along with the occasional moose, I've often flushed grouse from the aspens along the springs. On one glorious afternoon, Candy flushed a grouse from a clump of willows at the top of the knoll. It flew in a straight path, giving me a fast shot. With one bird in the vest, Candy returned to the willows and flushed another grouse and all of a sudden I had two birds in the bag.

More typical of Watercress Covert hunts is the day Candy flushed a grouse from the aspens next to the springs. I took a hurried shot, but the bird kept flying. No more birds flushed, so I leaned my gun against a tree and went to the water to collect a bag of salad. I filled my bag and went back to my gun. I got there just in time for a grouse to flush from the top of the tree on which I had leaned my gun. The bird was long gone by the time I had my gun to my shoulder.

A couple other coverts have drab names. There's the Upper Draw, for an aspen hillside just below the Continental Divide. The Big Draw is a canyon that seems almost limitless. About once a year, I take what I call the Long Walk, climbing to the top of a mountain ridge and following that ridge for several miles and dropping down to the creek level for the return trip. I've had a lot more action, over the years, in the creek bottom but I've also collected both blue grouse and ruffed grouse from the brush patches along the top of the ridge.

Sometimes, getting down off the ridge at the head of the canyon is a challenge. The first time I tried it, Alix and I followed a grouse into a side draw that came up the side of the canyon to near the top of the ridge. I got down and worked myself into a spot where the trail led to a drop-off and I had to hang on to a tree branch with one hand while I tried to figure where my next step was going to be. Just then, the grouse took off with an explosive flush. I couldn't do anything except rail at it.

I'm not convinced that my Montana grouse coverts are as good as the North Dakota coverts I left behind back in the '80s. But I've had many good days and in a good season, I'll add another valley or two to my collection of grouse coverts. If they're good, or have enough character, I'll even give them a name.

As for those coverts back in northeastern North Dakota, someday before I die, or worse, get too old to hunt, I hope to return.

Chapter 26

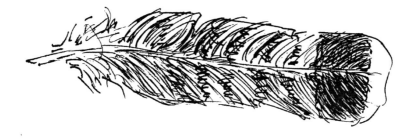

A Christmas Walk

It's almost time for my Christmas walk. After a big Christmas dinner it's good to go for a walk to settle the food and enjoy the lights of the early evening.

Those Christmas walks go back a long way in my memories. Many of our Christmas traditions seem to have special meaning for people who grow up on a farm or ranch. There's an old tradition, for example, that at midnight on Christmas Eve, farm animals are able to talk. For some reason, I've never heard of anybody actually catching their cows or sheep in the actual act of talking to each other, but perhaps the animals are too shy to show off their talents when people are around.

Still, we remember that at the first Christmas when Mary gave birth to the baby Jesus in a Bethlehem stable, animals witnessed the event. Later that night, shepherds from the hills around Bethlehem, perhaps accompanied by some of their sheep, came to worship the infant. It would have been a simple gathering; a carpenter and his young wife and baby, attended by shepherds, surrounded with the rich odors of the barn.

The barn of my youth probably didn't smell much different from that Bethlehem stable and likely Joseph made occasional excuses to step outside for fresh air. After helping my dad finish evening chores, I enjoyed taking a walk away from the farm buildings to clear my head and look at the stars appearing in the evening sky and reflected in the crystals of newly fallen snow.

The countryside of my youth was much darker than now. We didn't have the mercury vapor lights that now mark every rural home. The lights I'd see on my Christmas Eve walks came from either the sky or from neighboring farm homes, with occasional colored lights from a Christmas tree in a distant window.

Times change, of course. That farmhouse, to which I returned after my Christmas Eve walk, was bulldozed away and replaced over 40 years ago, several years after I married and left home to pursue a career. The last time I drove past my old home, I was surprised to see that even the barn and other outbuildings had disappeared, replaced by an expanse of green lawn.

Some things remain similar. A black Labrador retriever will go along with me on my evening walk. She doesn't look much like some of the cattle dogs of varied pedigree most of us had on farms, that we generally referred to as 'shepherds.' For many years, we had Buddy, a Great Pyrenees, a wooly white bear of a dog that, incidentally, added white hair to the gene pools of many shepherd pups born on neighboring farms. Dogs of any background share a common need and desire to spend as much time as possible with their humans and a Christmas evening stroll in an urban neighborhood is almost as good as a walk across a farm field.

On our walk, we'll see homes surrounded by parked cars, signifying a family get-together to celebrate the Christmas holiday. It reminds me of past Christmases in the "lutefisk ghetto" of southern

Minnesota where people with extended and entangled family lines incurred and discharged social obligations on a nightly basis throughout the Christmas season. These were nights where the familiar odors of manure-spattered boots and overalls hanging by the back door competed with the equally pungent scents of lutefisk and rutabaga coming from a steaming kitchen.

With changes in our lives, some things remain constant. We'll enjoy the crisp air of a December night and the crunch of snow under our steps. We'll take time to reflect on the passing of another year and of the many events that shape our lives. I'll note the fact that most of the people I remember from those Christmases of years past have probably been dead for years—an uncomfortable reminder of our own approaching mortality.

The tug of a leash brings me back to the present. We can take lessons from our dogs. They don't waste time reminiscing about the past. Each day is a new adventure and a search for new experiences. I do wonder, though, what's happening in a dog's mind when you see a sleeping dog's feet moving and hear soft yips. Are the dogs dreaming about pheasants or rabbits? We can only wonder.

And that, perhaps, is the greatest gift of a walk through a peaceful night in a war-torn world: a renewed sense of wonder at the miracle of Christmas.

Part Four

Final Thoughts

Chapter 27

Training the Pooch

"Train your dog yourself?"

When someone asks me that question I'm never quite sure whether it's a compliment or an accusation. My wife would likely suggest that it's an accusation, and If pressed I'd probably plead guilty.

Except for our early marriage years when living in apartments didn't seem compatible with dog ownership I've always lived with dogs, ranging from farm dogs of uncertain lineage, Shep, our German shepherd that went in the Army K9 Corps, and Buddy, a Great Pyrenees that helped me grow up, to four different Labrador retrievers that have enriched our last 40 years.

I didn't have much to do with training the dogs of my youth. My dad would have done most of what little training might have been considered needed. None of those dogs ever came in the house so we never worried about potty training or house breaking. I do remember taking Buddy on walks with a leash because a feed store in my home-town once sponsored a pet parade to help promote sales of their dog food, and my parents let me enter Buddy in the parade. I recall winning a ribbon for having the biggest dog.

With each of our bird dogs I've spent abundant amounts of time turning these pups into decent citizens. There is no doubt in my mind that spending lots of time with your pup is the most important part of dog training. Your dog wants to be part of a family and there's probably nothing more important than to make that dog a part of the family.

Our Labs have clearly been members of the family, each with distinct personalities and special relationships with family members. They have all been enthusiastic hunters and retrievers. When past dogs reached the end of their life span we grieved for them as much as for departed human loved ones.

At the same time, as my wife would freely point out, and she does so with some frequency, they have hardly been paragons of obedi-ence. In addition they often look expectantly, often with a bit of drool hanging from their jaw, while I'm eating dinner. They know from past experience that there may be rewards. When we've come to those in-evitable periods of transition, my wife has threatened, "Our next dog isn't going to get treats from the table." I've learned to keep my mouth shut and my wife has given up on me as a lost cause especially when I point out she frequently makes extra scrambled eggs for breakfast to share with the dog.

So, don't expect me to come up with any new insights into dog training.

Still, beginning with what is now an old, tattered and dog-eared edition of one of the classics of retriever training, "Training Your Retriever," by James Lamb Free, I've managed to accumulate a small library of books on training retrievers or other sporting dogs. I've also subscribed to *Gun Dog* magazine (as well as other outdoor publications) for many years and have picked up lots of training tips from them. There is even a "training for dummies" book in the mix.

I suspect you could take any of these books and stick to the basic training principles and you'll do just fine, though I can't help but think of one of the gurus of dog training who wrote a number of books on dog training. My son once had a conversation with a professional trainer who grumbled, "I knew him; I knew his dogs. He couldn't train a starving dog to eat meat."

Lest you say the same about me, I'm not about to write a book on dog training. Likewise I'm not going to spend a lot of time and ink writing about dog training. There are professionals who make their living training dogs and writing about dog training. They write books and magazine articles. They know what they're doing and get results.

I will, however, suggest that some standard training ideas be underlined and highlighted.

If you're starting a puppy fresh from the litter, don't waste your time with paper training. That's a principle I learned from James Lamb Free. Train the pup to do his business outside. Otherwise, you're likely to find a puddle on the Sunday paper.

Give your dog proper housing. In the house that means a crate or portable kennel. Pup may not appreciate it at first but they learn to love having that little space all their own. We're often amused when Flicka is in the house and occasionally gives us a funny look, as if to say, "You people are so boring," and then traipses off to go nap in her crate downstairs. That crate is also a big help in potty training. Pup doesn't want to mess in his or her bed, so they'll learn to hold it when they're in the crate. We actually have two crates. One stays in the house and the other, a bit smaller, just fits in the backseat of our car. Wherever we may be we can take her little bit of home along and you'd be surprised how often, when we're visiting, that she'll go to her crate for some peace and quiet.

If you have the yard space, get a kennel and put it on a concrete slab with a doghouse that the pup can get into to get out of the weather. A local fence company can likely supply you with a kennel of any size. The kennel we have is 10 feet by 4 feet and we've now had it for 40 years and four dogs and it will be good for another 40 years at least. We've moved it a couple times and poured new concrete slabs for it a couple times as well. A dog that's in a kennel isn't going to be prowling the neighborhood, getting into garbage, chasing cars, or getting pregnant without permission.

With both the crate and the kennel, the pup may whine and object to being confined in a kennel. Don't worry about hurting pup's delicate feelings. They'll get used to it and learn to love it.

In fact, dogs love routine in their lives. That's another basic training principle. Expose your pup to lots of variety in life when they're still young, so they learn that just about everything you do is plumb normal, whether it's going for walks, taking a ride in the car, spending long hours in the kennel, meeting people and other dogs, and, of course, hunting.

If I've been a success at turning puppies into hunting partners it's because I try to do lots of hunting and we've started pups hunting at a young age. I started taking both Candy and Flicka hunting when they were little pups. They learned the scent of pheasants and ducks, the excitement of a flushing pheasant and the 'boom' of a shotgun. They also got retrieving fever from chasing down crippled ducks. They also learned to not be afraid of getting wet. The prospect of chasing down a crippled bird is too exciting to worry about getting wet.

In fact, I recall a column in *Field & Stream* by the late Bill Tarrant, for many years the hunting dog editor for *F&S*. He wrote about a family in Idaho that, for several generations, bred and trained Chesapeake Bay Retrievers. Some of the older people said that for many of those years they didn't really do much formal training. "We just kept taking them out and they kind of figured things out."

I'll also suggest that you follow another time-proven technique and that's to train your dog to come to a whistle. If you ever watch a retriever field trial you'll see dogs, after a single whistle blast, whirl around and sit and then look for hand signals for where to go next. I've never remotely approached that level of training, but all my dogs have learned to at least come to a whistle. If you're outside on a windy day your voice or "pucker" whistle won't carry far, but your dog will hear your training whistle. Unless you're an opera singer a whistle is a lot more audible at long range than your voice. Trust me on this. It's

also easier on you. Otherwise you'll be like the guy I hooked up with for part of a day in Iowa years ago. He had a good-looking English pointer that was a good bird finder but he conceded, "I can't hunt more than half a day anymore; I get too hoarse."

There are lots of whistles out there, and if you buy what looks like a standard referee whistle from the dog training rack at your pet supply store it'll do the job. Put it on a lanyard that hangs from your neck. It'll make you look like a real dog trainer. I've never tried using a "silent" whistle that supposedly is above a human's hearing range. Frankly, if I'm whistling at my dog and I'm being ignored, I'd like to at least have the satisfaction of knowing that my whistle is making some kind of noise.

I have several whistles, one of which hangs in our camping trailer as a spare that always goes along on the trip. That one is one of the standard training whistles, the Acme Thunderer. I'll just mention that if you get one of those, be careful. You can damage your own hearing with it.

Electronic collars are, to many, a sensitive topic. Not all dogs need it. Some dogs do. Flicka was one of them. She figured out at an early age that she could run faster than I can and, therefore, if she was off her leash she could do whatever she felt like doing, even when it was potentially life-threatening. We called her the Monster Mutt. Really. I finally ordered a collar and after a couple weeks use she became a model citizen. During her first few seasons I always used the collar on hunting outings as a remote control on her if she was ranging too far out. The last couple seasons I quit charging it because she didn't need that kind of remote control anymore; the whistle usually worked. Don't be afraid of using an electronic collar, but follow the directions.

So, there's my insight into dog training. Feed and house your puppy, get a good book or two on training and follow the directions. And whatever you do, take your pup out in the outdoors to learn about live birds and hunting.

I also suggest that if you have thoughts about field trials or other competition, you'd be well off signing up your pup with a professional trainer.

Oh, and if you take your dog hunting early and often, I won't say anything if you occasionally slip him a bite of steak.

Chapter 28

Transitions

The season started well.

Montana's upland bird season begins on September 1 and at daybreak Candy and I started our first walk of the season across the top of the mountain in search of blue grouse.

This particular mountain has two knobs at its top, with a forest road dividing the two peaks. We began our walk at the lower knob where the year before we had flushed several grouse from a meadow, collecting one of them, on our way to getting a legal limit of three birds.

This time, we didn't find any grouse so we walked over to the other knob, circling through the timber and coming out on the other side so we could circle our way back to the truck with the bright morning sun at my back, rather than squinting into the sun.

We were walking along the sidehill in light sagebrush cover below the treeline. Candy picked up a scent and started following the trail down the hill. I'm watching her, debating whether to turn downhill when a grouse flushed at my feet. I have an easy going-away shot at the bird and a moment later I pocket the chunky mature grouse in my vest.

A minute later, several more grouse flush and I'm able to scratch one down. Candy is on the bird for the retrieve. It's just 8:30 and we have two grouse.

That's all the action we have that morning, and we're back in camp for breakfast by 10 a.m.

We made that same drive up the mountain every day for the first five days of the season and we got into grouse every morning (and trout every evening), and when we got home I felt fortunate to be able to put half a dozen blue grouse in the freezer.

I went fishing the following weekend, but the weekend after that we got in a couple days of camping, fishing and grouse hunting. This turned out to be a rainy weekend and while Candy put up one ruffed grouse for two flushes the only thing I got was wet.

Fortunately, the fishing was productive, even if all the fish seemed to be 8-inch rainbows. I began thinking of that weekend's fishing as "the attack of the silver midgets."

If the fishing produced no lunkers and the hunting no birds, it was still a celebratory weekend, as Kay and I observed our 44th wedding anniversary.

Our next hunt, a week later, was just after the autumnal equinox, meaning weather forecasts for rain likely meant snow in higher elevations. I decided I'd better get out before a predicted storm system moved in.

It was raining lightly when Candy and I started our walk up the creek bottom.

About 15 minutes into our walk Candy is getting excited about bird scent. Seconds later a grouse flushes from the willows and I get a quick crossing shot. I drop the bird, a small grouse, likely from a late hatch, with tiny little tailfeathers. It's the first ruffed grouse of the season, so the hunt is already a success.

We continued up the creek bottom, finally getting to the creek's source far up the mountainside. We walk across the mountainside to the next branch of the creek, following the aspens back down the canyon.

Candy is working ahead of me and I'm surprised when I see a grouse materialize in front of me, on the ground. The bird flies up to a tree branch. I'll confess I've shot a few grouse out of trees over the years, though every year I vow to reform and take only flying shots. Candy has returned and she picks up the scent wafting down from the tree branch. With both a human yelling, and a dog looking at the bird with interest, the grouse decides things are getting too stressful and flies off. My record on grouse flushing from a tree isn't good, but this time I drop the bird with one shot. This bird is a nearly full-grown brown-phase grouse.

Next, we work into a side draw that goes up the hillside. I'm startled when I see a grouse flush and fly, out of range, up the hill. A moment later another grouse flushes, giving me a quick shot that I miss. As I quicken my pace up the hillside, hoping for a re-flush, another grouse flushes from the edge of the aspens. I get off a quick shot, and while I don't see the bird fall I have this gut feeling that I'd better check this one further. Candy and I climb out of the aspens and start climbing the hillside when we see a lightly wounded grouse running back down the hill for the safety of the aspens. Candy is on her immediately and we have our limit of ruffed grouse.

I check my watch. It's just 11 a.m. We got our limit of ruffed grouse in a two-hour walk—though it's a 20-minute hike to get back to the truck and my pants and boots are well-soaked after trudging through the sodden cover.

It snowed the next day, but it didn't last long. The following Wednesday, a brilliant, sunny day, with clear blue skies contrasting the yellows and golds of the aspens, we went for an afternoon hunt. I'm carrying my Canon SLR to pick up some fall foliage photos.

We work through one covert, moving a grouse that flushes, unseen. We move down to the Watercress Covert where Candy puts up another grouse, a mature brown-phase bird. I get the bird on my second shot.

We don't move any more birds and, unfortunately, I forget to bring a plastic bag with me, so I'm not able to bring home a watercress salad. I'm not too worried about it, however. I expect to return in following weeks.

The next afternoon, after spending several hours in front of the computer, I decide to take a break from writing and give Candy some exercise. We run into our neighbor from across the street who is throwing tennis balls for his German shorthair. This is a game that Candy loves and in one of her merry chases for the tennis ball she suddenly stops, holding up her left rear leg.

I have this sinking feeling of déjà vu. This seems altogether too similar to last year's North Dakota pheasant hunt that ended with Candy holding up her right rear leg.

A couple days later, the veterinarian confirms our tentative diagnosis. Yes, she has ruptured the other ACL. The doctor suggests more knee surgery.

Kay and I are in a quandary and we decide to take no action. We have been half expecting this day, as a year before the veterinarian who did Candy's first knee surgery said, "You have to think of this as the first of two procedures. It's my experience that when a dog blows an ACL, the chances are the other one will go within a year."

While we've had a good month of hunting, we noticed that Candy, just eight years old this past summer, has aged considerably this past year. After each of those early season outings Candy spent the next couple days resting. We were reluctant to put her through more surgery, especially if it ages her as much as her first surgery did.

We tell the veterinarian that we'll elect no treatment at the present time, other than getting a prescription for a painkiller.

A week later we're in eastern Montana for the opening of the pheasant season. We considered staying home. During the week an unusually early snowstorm raged across the Great Plains, dumping wet, heavy snow on the prairies. Interstate 94 was closed from Miles City to Bismarck, North Dakota. Along with the weather, we had a dog still suffering from the initial trauma of a ruptured ACL. The river bottom cover we hunt on opening weekend is tough on both hunters and dogs and would be too hard for Candy to hunt.

On top of that, in the post-Hurricane Katrina gas crunch, a gallon of regular topped out at $2.899 (little did we realize that a couple years later gas would go over $4 a gallon and we'd figure we'd died and gone to heaven with $2.90 a gallon prices). This is not going to be an inexpensive trip, pulling a camping trailer across Montana with a gas-guzzling truck.

We finally decide to make the trip across the state. My entire being is in turmoil over the disability of my hunting partner, but I remind myself that I hunted pheasants before I ever had a dog and I guess that I can do it again if I have to, though I have some more second thoughts about the whole thing when we gas up in Billings. The truck was running on empty when we limped into a gas station and it cost almost $70 to top off.

Nevertheless, we make it to Glendive, Kay's hometown. We're camping in a city park, convenient to her sister's home. There are patches of snow all around in the park, along with tree branches that snapped off during the week's snowstorm. Lois, Kay's sister, reports that some city streets are all but impassable because of fallen branches.

On opening day I'm up bright and early, and after reluctantly leaving Candy in the trailer with Kay, I'm off to the farm. After a visit with the farm family, catching up with events of the year, and commiserating over the cold, wet weather of the week that has put a halt to sugar beet harvest, I leave the house and park the truck at the edge of the field where I'm assigned to hunt.

The cover is soggy from the week's snowy weather and there are patches of snow here and there. The skies are clearing, however, so it should be a nice day.

After 35 years of hunting with Labrador retrievers, it takes some mental adjustment to hunting alone. I try to recall what I used to do, and that is to move through the cover slowly, making frequent stops, hoping that a pheasant will get nervous and take to the air. The technique worked years ago and it still works, though I wonder how many birds I'm walking by as I trudge through the weed patches.

By 10 a.m., I've had shots at just two pheasants. Luckily, I dropped those two pheasants with two shots, with each falling dead in thin cover. I need one more pheasant for my limit of three.

I re-work cover I worked earlier, missing a few shots. A low point is when I go into a strip of trees, brush and weeds between a creek and an irrigation canal. I step over a fallen tree and suddenly I collapse to the ground with charley horses in both legs. After about 10 minutes the cramps have subsided and I gingerly get back up to get back into the hunt.

At a point where the creek makes a 45-degree bend a pheasant flushes but I don't have time for a shot. Then another rooster flushes and I get off a long shot. I think I might have touched it but I see the bird fly off, eventually disappearing over a distant hillside. Then a third rooster flushes and I drop this one into heavy cover the other side of the creek.

I try not to think that if Candy were along she'd be on her way to retrieve the bird. This time, I have to work myself out of the cover and cross the creek at a culvert and then try to find where the bird had dropped five minutes earlier. I wasn't optimistic.

As I approach the weed patch where the bird dropped, I'm surprised to see the pheasant standing up, next to a fence, apparently trying to figure its next options. I didn't hesitate. I raised my gun, held just over the top of the bird's head and shot. For once I did it just right. The pattern clipped the top of the bird's head and at 2 p.m. I had my limit of birds for the day.

During the middle of the night I awake to the sound of rain falling on the trailer roof. Ordinarily it's a good sound, guaranteed to put people to sleep. Tonight it just meant that hunting conditions, which had rapidly improved with yesterday's bright sunshine, would be deteriorating.

When I get to the farm the rain has slowed to a drizzle, and a few minutes into my hunt the rain has stopped. "Maybe it won't be so bad," I tell myself, as I hunt my way across a benchland overlooking the river bottoms toward a brushy draw that often holds birds.

As I get to the edge of the draw birds start flushing. I'm able to pick out a rooster that flushes at close range and it drops into the open. I walk over to get it, and after pocketing the bird I start back up the draw, picking up rocks and throwing them down into the thick stuff, hoping to flush some more birds. The birds start flushing out of range at the top of the draw. There are about a dozen pheasant roosters that make a successful escape. Obviously, this would have been a good time to have several hunters posted around the draw to hold the birds a little longer.

The rain has started again, so I make a circle back to the truck to put on another layer that, hopefully, will keep me dry a little longer.

I walk a line of trees along the creek and at a bend a rooster flushes, giving me a quick, but unsuccessful shot. There are a couple guys walking along the top of a railroad embankment on the other side of the creek. I walk in parallel with them, hoping they'll push something my way. No such luck.

I'm getting wetter and wetter with the cold, drenching rain that has, by now, soaked through my layers of clothing, so I make a circle back to the truck and start the engine and turn the heater on full blast. After about 10 minutes I decide I'll try one more walk before I give it up as a bad cause. This walk lasted only minutes before I decided I'd had as much fun as I could take. I returned to the truck and shed a couple layers of clothes and made a stop at the farmhouse to deliver a box of candy and say "Thanks," before going back to town.

We make the trip back to western Montana the next day. I figure that we spent something like $250 on gas this weekend, plus going out for dinner with Kay's sister and husband a couple times. Of course, by hauling a trailer we didn't have any motel expense, so we probably broke even. Still, considering the small amount of meat we'll get from four pheasants, we'd better enjoy our pheasant dinners.

It's yet another reminder that any thoughts that I'm providing for my family by pheasant hunting are just misguided self-justification.

I have a busy week at home after getting back from the trip, getting caught up on writing assignments and a hectic week of rehearsals (I play French horn in our community symphony) and a Saturday night concert.

Throughout the week, however, my thoughts are dominated with, let's be honest, self-pity. My dog is hurting and can't hunt, and everybody damn well better feel sorry for me—or something like that.

Still, we come to a decision. "Well, of course, we have to get a new dog," my wife says, encouraging me to start looking.

Our local newspaper has had want ads with Lab puppies all summer, but not now. I check the ads in *Gun Dog* magazine and start checking websites.

October isn't necessarily a good time to start puppy shopping. Most professional breeders gear things for late winter and spring litters.

Unfortunately, I seem to be out of sequence—and have been for years.

We bought Sam, our first black Lab, in late summer of 1970. I grew up with dogs and had wanted one all along, though living in rented apartments or houses, we weren't able to make the move. Kay's parents never cared for pets around the house so she grew up without dogs. In fact, Kay was a bit scared of dogs.

We bought our first house the previous winter when the job took us to Miles City, Montana. We decided, once summer came, that this was the time to get a puppy. We'd looked at different breeds and Kay finally laid down the law to me: "You can have any dog you want, as long as it's a Labrador retriever."

Sam was too young to hunt that first season, or so the thinking went at the time. She made up for it in following years. Sam spoiled us. She trained easily, was good with the kids, lived to retrieve birds, had a good nose, and had a wonderful soft mouth when handling birds.

We were back in North Dakota a few years later and Sam made the transition from sharptails and pheasants to water-fowl and we learned, together, about ruffed grouse.

After Kevin got into high school we started taking hunt-ing trips to the pheasant areas of North Dakota during the annual teacher's convention weekend. Those were good trips that cemented those already strong father/son bonds. When I think back to those years, I can't ignore the fact that parenthood can be challenging, especially when kids are going through puberty, but we never had a bad hunt.

It was on one of those hunts when, in late afternoon, I dropped a pheasant that landed running. Sam, then about age eight or so, took off after it. Kevin and I stood by and relaxed while we waited for Sam to come back with her prisoner. To our surprise, Sam came back huff-ing and puffing with no bird. Kevin looked at me gravely, noting the obvious, "She'd never miss an easy retrieve like that before."

Still, Sam never lost her love for hunting. In her last few years she'd have occasional seizures where she'd collapse, but after a few minutes rest, would bounce back up and resume hunting. Once, when she was about 12, she collapsed on a warm September afternoon's hunt. This time, I didn't think she'd make it. In fact, I drove my Scout into the field where she'd fallen and I loaded her into the vehicle. I was convinced she was dying, and the least I could do was take her to a cool and comfortable spot. I drove to a wooded hillside overlooking one of the creek bottoms where we hunted ruffed grouse.

I carried her out of the truck and gently laid her down on the grass. A cool breeze rustled the branches overhead. I sat down next to her and quietly cried as I tried to work up my courage to get my shotgun to end Sam's suffering. I don't remember how long I sat there with her, but all of a sudden, Sam sat up, looked around and then barked, as if to ask, "So, what's your problem?"

After this brush with death, the next couple months were possibly the sweetest season we had together. Sam couldn't handle long days in the field, but with her patience and experience made some of her best retrieves. I recall one October morning we approached a prairie pothole and flushed a bunch of mallards. I swung my Weatherby pump gun and shot three times and three ducks hit the water—my first and only honest "triple" I've ever made. A couple ducks fell in heavy cover, but Sam patiently and persistently found all three ducks.

Sam's last hunt was on Columbus Day of 1984, a holiday from work. It was one of those golden days of bright sunshine and fall colors. We went to a couple of our favorite grouse coverts. I don't recall that we flushed any grouse that day, and for the most part Sam was content to trudge along at my heels. Still, she had that sensitive nose. We were walking across a field to an aspen and oak creek bottom when Sam suddenly surged ahead and flushed a covey of Hungarian partridge. I was so surprised that I didn't even shoot. On our last walk of the day we watched a flock of wild turkeys feed in a field next to the aspens.

I didn't go hunting that following Saturday. The Scout had brake problems and was scheduled to go into the shop the next week. Kay told me in no uncertain terms that I wasn't driving out of town with bad brakes. I moped around the house all day, as it was an ideal autumn day for hunting.

Late in the afternoon, I had steaks on the grill and Kay and I were sitting on the back steps of the house, enjoying late afternoon sunshine. Sam was romping in the yard, prompting Kay to comment, "She still thinks she's a puppy."

The next morning I was up early for a church trip. I went downstairs to let Sam out. Sam always slept on a rug in the basement laundry room. Instead of meeting me at the door all was silent. Sam lay still, stiff and cold. She had died during the night.

We carried her outside and put her lifeless body in the garage, as I had to leave.

I'm afraid I had trouble concentrating on church business that morning, as I quietly grieved.

That afternoon, back from my trip, I dug a grave in the garden. Rain was falling as I wrapped Sam in an old blanket and put her in the ground. I put a few pheasant and grouse tailfeathers next to her gray muzzle before I started shoveling dirt over her still body.

Sam's death marked a milestone in our lives. I was 30 when she became a part of our family, and our children were in elementary school. When we called Kevin and Erin to tell them our sad news, Erin was a college sophomore and Kevin was at graduate school at the University of Illinois. Kay and I were approaching our mid-40s.

I didn't do much hunting that fall. I was chairman of a call committee for our church, and our search for a pastor took up most of my free time.

After Thanksgiving, I made a trip to western North Dakota. I needed at least one pheasant hunt.

It was an unseasonably mild and sunny weekend, more like October than late November. It felt strange to be walking fields where, in past seasons, Sam had some of her best hunts. I approached a brush patch where I remembered Sam flushing and retrieving a pair of pheasant roosters a couple years earlier.

A pheasant flushed and I shot, dropping the bird, but it seemed an impossible job finding the pheasant in the heavy cover.

I finally found the bird, but not until I broke down in tears, standing out on the open prairie and saying, over and over again, "Oh Sam, Sam, why did you have to leave me."

Those months after Sam died were a time strangely without canine responsibilities.

There's an apocryphal story of when now-retired Supreme Court Associate Justice Sandra Day O'Connor was going through her Senate confirmation hearings. A senator was trying to pin her down on *the* controversial issue of the past decades, and was grilling her on her views on when life begins.

According to the story, Ms. O'Connor squelched further questions by responding, "Life begins after 40, after the kids leave home and the dog dies."

Though I guess my wife and I were still young enough we had no intentions of having more children, though the thought of not getting another dog never occurred to us.

We had our period of grieving for Sam, and it was time to move on.

Alix was one of a large litter of little brown puppies. The mother's owner had graduated from college the previous spring and immediately got a chocolate Lab puppy, and then had her bred right away. The young man's basement apartment had one room set aside as a nursery, with all the smells and sounds you might expect. I think it was getting to him, as he mentioned, while we wrote our check for the puppy, that the remaining pups from the litter were going to a local pet store the next day. I suspect he may have had some hints from his landlord along those lines.

As we drove away the pup started whining. "Oh no," I said, "We don't want a whiner. Let's take her back." I was joking, of course, but the pup, which we named Alix, never forgot how to whine.

Alix always knew when I had an outing planned; whether it was hunting or fishing made no difference. I'd try to make my advance preparations when she was out of the house or curled up, sleeping, in the living room. Still, it never failed. When I got up in the morning I'd hear Alix whining from her cage in the flytying room downstairs. Any other day of the week, when I'd be up early and getting ready to go to work, she'd be quiet and patient until I was ready to go down and bring her up. How she infallibly knew when I was putting on boots instead of a coat and tie I'll never understand.

In the fall of 1997, we could tell she was slowly dying, though she still had a few good hunts left in her.

Alix's last real hunt was on the Friday before Thanksgiving. My friend, John Banovich, and I were out in pursuit of ducks. We hit one of our reliable spots, a tract of public land along the Beaverhead River. The river makes a horseshoe bend and there are quiet eddies where ducks often shelter.

I'm trudging through heavy brush, along with thin ice left from when the river flooded from earlier ice jams on the river. Both Alix and Candy, not quite four months old, are with me. As I approach one spot that looks like it might shelter ducks, I see ducks flush from across the river. Then, as I got closer, a dozen ducks flushed. I picked out a drake mallard and shot, dropping the duck. I broke my gun open to reload and while I'm standing there fumbling with shotgun shells, what seemed like a thousand ducks flushed from in front of me. There's just a solid wall of mallards, with green heads and blue wing speculums flashing in the November sunlight. All I can do is stand there, mouth open, thinking, "Holy shit!"

After the birds are gone I think, "I should have shot," or "I should have had a camera."

With the birds gone, Alix trudged out to the water, wading a couple feet into the river, and came back with my duck.

A few minutes later, a pheasant flushed from my feet. I got off a couple quick shots, but the bird had its afterburners on and was gone.

Over lunch, I told John about all the ducks we put up along the river. John asks, "How many did you get?"

I had nothing to say. How do you tell a fellow hunter that it never occurred to me to shoot?

The following week we went to North Dakota for the Thanksgiving holiday and I shelled out for a non-resident license so that Kevin and I could hunt together. Though Alix was anxious to go she was clearly too weak for pheasant hunting.

Alix did go on one more hunt. On December 4, John and I went out again. We made a successful sneak on a little creek and we each dropped a duck. Alix retrieved John's duck, which fell in the open, but didn't have strength to wade across the muddy creek bottom to get my duck, which was on the edge of the water in a little corner.

This was Alix's last hunt. A few days later, Alix stayed home when Candy retrieved her first duck, and by the end of the day retrieved three of the five ducks we brought home. A couple days later, Candy had a banner day, retrieving a total of five ducks and two Hungarian partridge.

My hunting log tells of more hunts in the next few weeks, but Alix isn't part of it. She is clearly deteriorating. She's constipated much of the time because she can't tolerate enough exercise to get her bowels moving properly. She spends most of her time sleeping, often so soundly it's hard to wake her up. Just about every morning, when I go downstairs to get her up, I can't help but wonder if she's still alive, and secretly hope that she might have died during the night, like Sam did, and spare us the decision.

On the night of January 21, 1998, three weeks short of her 13th birthday, Alix collapsed when I took her and Candy outside to potty before bedtime. I came back in to tell Kay that Alix had collapsed and was dying. We called our veterinarian's answering service and a few minutes later the vet called back. I said, "Alix collapsed and is dying, and we don't want her to suffer." He said he'd meet us at his clinic. We loaded Alix up in the truck for one last ride. At the clinic, the veterinarian slipped a hypodermic needle into a vein. Alix drifted off to sleep and a moment later was still.

When we got home, Candy sat up in her cage, probably wondering what we'd been doing. I said, "Okay, girl, you're in charge of the dog department. Are you ready?"

It seems all too short a time from that sad night to the present when all of a sudden we were in the puppy market again; and, again, in the middle of the hunting season.

Kevin sent an email reporting that the Minot *Daily News* had an ad for puppies that sounded promising. He called on Saturday, reporting that both the litter's parents came from pointing Lab lines. The pups seemed intelligent and well-behaved. Somehow, it felt right. We told Kevin to contact the breeder and tell him we'd take one of the last two females he had left.

We tell Kevin we'll come to Minot the following weekend. In the meantime, we continued with previous plans to go hunting along the Rocky Mountain Front. We hoped Candy would be able to tolerate some hunting on the prairies.

We arrived at the farm in early afternoon. Our friend, Bill, is a retired county extension agent but spends much of his time on the family farm his grandfather homesteaded some 95 or so years ago. It's arid country but irrigation has made it pheasant friendly. An irrigation canal carries life-giving water from the Sun River to area farms and ranches. On Bill's farm, the canal cuts across an open hillside. During the irrigation season the water saturates the soil along the ditch banks and percolates down the slopes. In some spots, the ground is spongy with water and clumps of willows, cattails and other cover have grown up. Bill grazes cattle through the winter, but they tend to stay away from the soggy areas, giving pheasants some quality habitat.

I've had some fast hunting on the property and some slow hunting, as well. I recall a couple years ago when I collected a couple limits of pheasants. This afternoon the pheasants were scarce. I had a shot (successful) at just one rooster, though Candy did put up a couple hens and one rooster that was out of range.

The next day I went to another farm, the site of great hunts over the years. The property is just 160 acres, with farm buildings in one corner. An irrigation ditch cuts through the middle of the quarter, and there's another corner with trees, brush and a cattail slough. The owners use the farm as, basically, one big field, growing wheat or barley every year. Pheasants love it because they can feed on waste grain all fall and winter and have brushy areas for shelter.

There has been a new element the last couple years. They lease out grazing to a neighboring rancher. With the cows comes another problem: electric fences. I don't argue with it because they fence off the farmstead and the better wildlife habitat from the cows. Unfortunately, it does make it difficult for Candy. She's trying to follow the lines of cover and a couple times she gets zapped when the wire touches her back. She yelps in pain but doesn't know what has happened. About all I can do is have her at my side and then hold the wire up with my gun while she goes under the wire.

We work our way into the magic corner where, not surprisingly, pheasants flush and disappear, screened by dense willow trees. I can't worry about those birds, however. I'm confident we'll find more.

We work our way into tall grass at the edge of a willow patch and birds begin flushing. I pick out a rooster and drop it with my first shot. Candy runs over and I'm expecting her to come back with the bird. It's as if the bird has disappeared into thin air. We both search the area and we finally have to give up the bird as lost.

We double back and work the outside of the line of trees we just came through when a rooster flushes. I barely have a glimpse of it through the tree branches, but it's enough to see colors and I shoot. It's a difficult shot, but I hear the bird drop with a thump. Candy is on it immediately and I pocket the bird.

We put up another bird on the edge of the cattail slough and I drop that and Candy is able to find it right away.

We walk through the brushy area some more and while we put up a couple hens, the roosters seem to have moved out, so we move out also, following a weedy drainage ditch along the edge of the field and follow that until we get to the irrigation ditch that cuts through the middle of the field.

We follow the irrigation ditch and hens start flushing from the cover along the ditch. We continue walking and finally a rooster flushes. It's a tough, quartering away shot. I miss with the bottom barrel but the bird drops like a stone after I touch off the top barrel. We've gotten our limit of pheasants in a two-hour walk.

Later that afternoon I'm back to camp and I take my bucket of dressed pheasants up to Bill's house to finish cleaning them at his outside hydrant. Walking back to our trailer I chat with Bill, who's tinkering with some machinery. He mentions that he saw a covey of Huns fly into grassy cover at the top of a knoll behind him.

While Candy was thoroughly tired out from our pheasant hunt, she was ready to go as soon as I got back to the trailer with my bucket of birds and got my shotgun out from the back of the truck. We walked back up the draw towards Bill's house and darned if I didn't see the covey of Huns fly across from one knoll to another. There's nothing like knowing exactly where the birds are.

Candy and I walk up the hillside, which looks totally empty and barren. Suddenly, the air is full of birds as the covey flushes with a rush of wings and chirps. I pick out a bird and shoot—and miss. I shoot again but miss again, and the hillside is, again, empty. My record with Huns isn't great.

The next morning Candy and I take another walk around the farm but see no pheasants; just a red fox that makes a quick about face after spotting us. In late morning, we break up camp and hit the road for home. We have traveling to do the next day.

* * * * *

Life can be full of surprises.

Imagine, if you will, that you're a Labrador retriever puppy. Life is good. You've got a good-looking mother and a big bruiser of a dad and a big yard for romping. True, things have been getting a little lonely, as, for some reason, all your brothers and sisters have been disappearing.

You don't really understand what happened with the siblings, but luckily, at your age you have a short memory and you just go with the flow.

Then it's Monday morning. You're out in the yard with Mom and your master when this car drives up and a man and woman get out. You run over to check them out. They seem okay, but then you go back to Mom and try to figure out what's going on.

It doesn't make a lot of sense, but you see these strangers exchange some pieces of paper with your master and then they pick you up and go for a ride in their car. Everybody in the car is making a fuss over you so maybe this could be a fun ride.

In a few minutes you're at a different house in another part of town. There are a couple dogs there and another big yard, so things aren't too bad. In the house is a black dog that looks a lot like Mom, though not as patient. There are kids and cats to chase, so, in spite of everything, this has been a fun day.

Then, just as you're ready for a good nap, you find yourself all alone in a crate. You're lonesome and you start yelling for some company and all of a sudden that strange man yells at you.

The next morning, when it's still dark and cold, the man takes you outside and then you get in the car, again, and many hours later you're at another house. You spend a couple hours exploring the house and then, all of a sudden, it's dark and you're back in the crate, again. You start telling the people you don't like being in the crate and then that mean old man comes and yells at you, again.

All you really know, at this point, is that life surely has gotten confusing.

And that is how a new hunting partner began learning about a new family and her new home.

At the suggestion of our daughter, this new pup acquired the name of Flicka—not after Flicka the horse, as some have suggested, but after Fredericka Von Stade, the opera singer, who is known throughout the music world as Flicka. The pup's official name, as registered with the AKC, is Velvet Marquesa Flicka Storm.

While we are dealing with the challenges of a new puppy in the house, Candy isn't through hunting.

A couple days after getting home with Flicka, Candy and I go out on a stormy Saturday morning for a ruffed grouse hunt. There are snowflakes in the air when we leave, but west of town it's almost a whiteout. I debate turning around and going home, but by the time I've gotten to a logical place to turn around we're out of the worst of the snow squall.

There's an inch of snow on the ground when we get to the wildlife management area, with occasional snow showers moving through.

In a two-hour hunt, with Candy's help I bag two ruffed grouse, both of which she had sniffed out and flushed and made the retrieve. We could have hunted longer but I didn't want to put further stress on Candy's bad knee, so I'm perfectly content to come home with two ruffs.

When we got home, I hid one of the grouse in a leaf pile and then we brought Flicka out to see if she'd find it. At first she didn't notice it, but when she did there was no hesitation. She picked up the bird and went tearing off with it. She likes it! Obviously, we're going to have to get that retrieving instinct under control.

The following weekend I went on a successful deer hunt, getting a fat forkhorn whitetail buck. The rest of the weekend was devoted to converting the deer to packages of frozen venison.

The next Friday was Veteran's Day, and Candy and I went hunting. The day started as a duck hunt. With Candy at my side, we walked a couple spring creeks in search of ducks. It was a mild day, what duck hunters often refer to as a "bluebird day." No ducks were in sight on the creeks and no birds were flying around.

From a grassy patch next to a slough, a pheasant flushed, just out of range. More pheasants flushed as I got closer and I took a long shot at one and missed. I stood there with an empty gun as several more pheasants, all roosters, flushed and made successful escapes.

"Candy, let's go see if we can find some more of those pheasants," I said, as we headed to the next field.

We walked through a patch of tall grasses and hen pheasants began flushing. I hoped that there might be a rooster in there, too, and at the very edge a cock pheasant flushed. I didn't get a good shot at the bird, but enough to scratch it down. Candy was on it immediately to prevent escape.

Candy picked up the scent of another pheasant in a weed patch and when the bird flushed I picked out the colors of a rooster and pulled the trigger. Candy quickly found the bird where it fell in high cover and brought it to me. We now had two pheasants in the vest. This was turning out to be a great hunt.

We were running out of pockets of cover when Candy put up yet another pheasant, a long-tailed bird with bright colors sparkling in the pale November sun. I shot and the pheasant hit the ground with a thump.

As we walked back to the truck I told Candy how proud I was of her. She's an 8-year-old dog with gimpy knees, but when it comes to finding pheasants in heavy cover, she's hard to beat.

It was a bittersweet moment when we shared a sandwich before heading for home. Candy is a heckuva bird dog, but with her bad knees, she probably shouldn't have been hunting at all. I was dreading the inevitable day when I'd leave her at home and start taking Flicka along on these hunts as my new hunting partner. It didn't seem that long ago when I first started taking Candy hunting, leaving another old Lab at home.

A week later we were in Oakland, California to spend Thanksgiving with our daughter, Erin, and her partner, Victoria. I'll spare you the Thanksgiving week negotiations, but when we headed home to

Montana, Candy stayed behind. Erin grew up with Sam, our first Lab, and has wanted one of her own for a long time, but with her work schedule, starting with a puppy would have been a challenge. They're a good pair. Back in college, over 20 years ago, Erin blew out a knee playing Frisbee, so between the two of them they have one good knee.

The trouble with having dogs is we know at the outset, when we bring that little puppy home that sooner or later they're going to break our hearts. Over the last eight years Candy and I shared many hunts and days along trout streams and in a better world we would be looking forward to at least several more years of outings together. But, she's living the dream of many: taking an early retirement and moving to California. Frankly, I had a hard time adjusting to life without my best friend. I wasn't ready to say goodbye, though I'm comforted in knowing that she's still in the family and we'll see her again.

It's also good to know that on Candy's last hunt we teamed up for one last limit of pheasants. She retired as a champion.

Post Script

The problem with dog stories is that they never have a happy ending.

Marley and Me, John Grogan's hilarious and best-selling story of his whacky yellow Labrador retriever, and *Merle's Door*, Ted Kerasote's story about the stray dog that adopted him, are examples of dog stories that keep the reader laughing until, of course, the bittersweet end.

At the end there are always tears.

When Candy was a pup, she had shown an early talent for digging holes in the yard, earning the nickname Digger. Back in the fall of 1997, after making the deal to acquire this new black puppy, as we got ready to leave, the breeder said, holding back a few tears, "Goodbye, Digger. Have a wonderful life."

As she snuggled into the lap of whoever wasn't driving, we discussed a name for the pup. It didn't take long before the name of Candy emerged—simply because she was so sweet.

As that fall gradually turned into winter, Candy started going along on hunting outings. By December, Alix stayed home and Candy, just four months old, took over as my bird dog. On December 8, Candy retrieved her first duck, and ended the outing with three retrieves. A couple days later she retrieved five ducks and two Hungarian partridge. We were thrilled with this precocious puppy.

As that hunting season ended, I wrote a note in my hunting diary, "She has an irrepressible personality, and is absolutely ding-dong nuts about retrieving. It's going to be fun seeing her develop as a maturing dog."

In the following years she learned about blue grouse, ruffed grouse, sharp-tailed grouse, and pheasants, as well as following me through the fishing season, though she was sometimes less than helpful, continually bringing me sticks to throw for her.

Whether we were hunting, fishing, or just going for a walk, she was always ready to go. She also developed a fetish for retrieving tennis balls, culminating with her greatest achievement when we took a vacation trip to the Oregon coast, where she somehow found a tennis ball in the Pacific Ocean.

Candy enjoyed retirement as an urban dog, living in a house with two women and three cats. Instead of hunting she went on daily walks in their wooded, hilly neighborhood, going to occasional wine tastings, and otherwise enjoying her new career. She drew admiring looks from many people for her look of athleticism as well as her friendly demeanor. Even the cats loved her.

Four and a half years later, Candy is an old, old dog; her hindquarters atrophying, and walking, even just standing, is difficult. We were in California for a visit with Erin and Victoria and we could see, in just a few days, continuing deterioration. Erin said she had perked up when we arrived, but then quickly went further downhill. The day after we left she made one last trip to the veterinarian for a little help on her way to her last great adventure.

Candy had great careers as a family member, bird dog, and happy retiree.

She had a wonderful life and we're the better for it.

I remember reading, years ago, of dog ownership as a long series of acquiring dogs and then having to say goodbye to them. Until, that is, we reach the point where finally a dog will have to say goodbye to us. Will Flicka be the one to have to say goodbye to me sometime during her life?

I'm not going to dwell on morbid thoughts. Flicka is now a seasoned veteran in the prime of life and I'm looking forward to many more seasons together as we wander the wetlands, prairies, and aspens. Her story, however, will wait for another day.

Post Script

Quantity discounts are available to your company or nonprofit
for reselling, educational purposes, subscription incentives, gifts and
fundraising campaigns. For more information, please contact the publisher.

Five Valleys Press
6240 Saint Thomas Dr
Missoula, Montana 59803
www.FiveValleysPress.com
info@fivevalleyspress.com

About the Author

Paul Vang grew up around dogs and pheasants on a farm in southern Minnesota. After graduating from St. Olaf College, Northfield, Minnesota, he had a 33-year career as a manager with the Social Security Administration. After leaving government service he launched a second career as a freelance writer and columnist.

In addition to weekly newspaper columns, his work has been published in many magazines, including *Montana Outdoors, North Dakota Outdoors, Kiwanis, Wheelin' Sportsmen, Blue Ridge*, and *Distinctly Montana*. He has won awards from the Outdoor Writers Association of America and Montana Newspaper Association. He's a past president of the Northwest Outdoor Writers Association.

Paul and his wife, Kay, and black Lab, Flicka, live in Butte, Montana—that is when he's not out hunting or flyfishing.

Illustrations are by the author's son, Kevin Vang. In his day job he's a professor of mathematics at Minot State University, Minot, North Dakota.